Warm Heritage

Warm Heritage

*Old Patchwork Quilts & Coverlets in
New Zealand and the Women
Who Made Them*

Pamela Fitz Gerald

David Bateman

Author's note on inch measurements

I have retained the use of imperial measurements, i.e., inches and feet, throughout this book for two reasons. First, the quilts were made at a time when imperial measurements were used. Second, because many quilting books and patterns come from the United States, where inches and feet are still used, most quilters still work in these measurements today.

Page 1: Log Cabin quilt made by Anna Hunger (see page 47).
Page 2: Detail of a Log Cabin crib quilt, from the collection of the Museum of Transport and Technology, Auckland (see pages 24-26).
Page 5: An example of a signature quilt (see pages 136-139), from the collection of the Waiouru Queen Elizabeth II Army Museum.

Publisher's note: Some quilts were not able to be moved for photography and so were photographed *in situ* by the author or owner. Although this has compromised the quality of the photographs, the quilts were felt to be important additions to New Zealand quilting heritage and so worthy of inclusion.

Copyright © Pamela Fitz Gerald, 2003
Copyright © David Bateman Ltd, 2003

Published 2003 by David Bateman Ltd,
30 Tarndale Grove, Albany, Auckland, New Zealand

ISBN 1-86953-529-4

Book Design by Roger Twinn of Twinn Image Ltd
Printed in China through Colorcraft Ltd

Acknowledgements

In working on the *Warm Heritage* project I have met many wonderful people eager to share their quilts and family histories. Sometimes I have almost felt the presence of the quiltmaker watching over me and delighting in my appreciation of their sewing skills. Occasionally discovering some of the interesting little personal touches these needlewomen gave to their quilts was an additional delight.

I am full of praise for the work of the photographer Anne Nicholas, who maintained such consistency in the standard she achieved when photographing the quilts, and being a sometime quilter herself I am sure did contribute to her enthusiasm in documenting the old charmers.

To all those quilt owners and museum personnel who have assisted me in finally getting this book into print I proffer my deepest thanks. I hope they will accept this as a personal appreciation of their help and not be disappointed in the length of the gestation period, which I sometimes felt was equating with that of a whole herd of elephants.

Pamela Fitz Gerald

Contents

Detail from a crazy quilt made by Euphemia Maxwell (see page 116).

Introduction

My search to find old patchwork quilts and coverlets in New Zealand started in the mid-1970s when my name and address, and that of another New Zealander, were given to a young American woman intending to visit our country. She and her husband wanted to look at New Zealand with the prospect of settling here (they lived in California on an earthquake fault line, 30 miles away from a nuclear power station and crime was on the rise) and while she was here she wanted to meet people with similar interests in quilts. She was a subscriber to *Quilter's Newsletter Magazine* and had contacted the editor to see if there were any subscribers in New Zealand; at that time (1976) there was me and one other New Zealand subscriber.

From reading *Quilter's Newsletter Magazine* since early 1975 I had found the articles that they published on old quilts fascinating. Realising that in the United States there were even museums (or parts of museums) devoted entirely to quilts I thought that my correspondent would be interested in seeing what we had in New Zealand (if anything). I immediately found more old quilts in Auckland than I expected, but hit a blank wall when seeking information from the various smaller museums in places which I fully expected to have examples of some of these treasures, for not one of them replied to my letters. Eventually

sufficient quilts were located to satisfy the interest of the expected traveller.

After her arrival, however, when my American friend and I travelled together to many parts of the North Island looking for and at old quilts (as well as the scenery) we were both rather disappointed. Few, if any, adequate records of the age of the quilts had been kept, or of who had actually made them. In most cases only the donor was named (though sometimes not even that) with perhaps a note saying the quilt was over 100 years old but no indication as to when it had reached its centenary. Often these old textiles had been inappropriately cared for, not only by, for the most part, the volunteer staff in small museums, but also in some more established museums by paid staff who we felt should have known better. For example, quilts were displayed on beds with the sun shining through a window directly onto them. In one case, plastic sheeting had been laid over the quilt to keep off the dust, ignoring the fact that moisture would form under the plastic and put the quilt in double jeopardy. A very old coverlet, once again displayed right by a window, had a rusty hat-pin holding the folds of the draped coverlet in place, with the added insult of a rusty safety-pin being used to attach its label.

The worst example of abuse I later found the

following year when I visited a medium-sized South Island museum. An elaborately made beautiful old quilt had been folded many times to make it small enough to be nailed all around the edge with metal carpet tacks to a piece of board, to act as a backdrop to a small table displaying various items of a Victorian lady's dressing table. In total these items probably were nowhere near the value of the old English quilt, which someone had obviously donated to preserve for younger generations to marvel at. The carpet tacks securing the folded quilt were of the sort with a three-sided shank, which meant that each tack had a point and three sharp edges cutting into the fabric.

Following the visit from the American and anticipating that she might be the forerunner of other quilt addicts, I decided to embark on a personal project to continue seeking out more quilts, photographing them and forming a sort of register of their whereabouts. Where possible I also wanted to find out their stories while there still might be people around who remembered the needlewomen who had made them, as I realised that this was an aspect of New Zealand women's history which was fast disappearing.

Over the following years every hint of the whereabouts of quilts was followed up, and annual holidays and long weekends were often taken travelling both islands to visit quilts and record as much as I could about them. Those in the care of families who had received them from earlier generations proved the most interesting in many cases as the inheritors could frequently provide the history of both the quilt and its maker.

Through the 1980s the project was put on hold, mostly because of work commitments and involvement in organising the first New Zealand National Patchwork and Quilting Symposium (held in December 1984), and, in early 1985, the Auckland Patchwork & Quilters Guild, which was formed immediately after the symposium. In 1983, however, I made an extended holiday visit to the United States and Canada, staying mainly with quilting friends. In North Carolina a symposium is held every year with each county or area taking their turn to host the event, and I received a lot of guidance from my friends there about organising our symposium. We also had many discussions about old quilts, for they were in the planning stages of establishing a research programme to document North Carolina's old quilts. In searching out and organising documentation days to record the over 10,000 old quilts that were located, the group had massive support from the state's many hundreds of quilters, who also helped with fundraising to add to the financial support being provided by the state. The quilts were documented and photographed, and all information was put onto microfiche for storing at the various museums.

By the time I made a second journey to America following my retirement in 1989, most of the other states, as well as North Carolina, had completed quilt documentation programmes. Knowing how significant their programme had been in recording a very important part of their social history, my particular friend in North Carolina, Erma Kirkpatrick, who is also a member of the prestigious American Quilt Study Group, was adamant that I should revive my own project. So, keen to set off again, I acquired from her copies of the three-page research questionnaire they used in their documentation programme and adapted it to be more appropriate to my needs. Many friends also pointed out that I should be putting a book together rather than a register. North Carolina and many other states had produced books to go along with their research work, as people were more interested in the personal stories and photographs than in information that they may already have known about quilts and quilting.

After looking over the American questionnaire, I realised that my early documenting of the fabrics and structural details of quilts had been far too cursory and that the quilts deserved to be rephotographed by a professional, unlike some of my earlier finds that I had photographed myself. During the 1990s, therefore, I did my best to make contact with and revisit the owners and caretakers of all the quilts on my 'register', and sought out other quilts I felt sure were being cared for by people I hadn't already contacted. I sent a circular to all the New Zealand patchwork and quilting clubs and guilds asking them to put out enquiries in their districts. I asked the clubs and guilds if they knew of any old quilts in their areas and asked if they could put up notices in places such as church noticeboards. I asked people to contact me if they could help and a few more quilts were unearthed. When I was contacted by the owners I would travel to them and make arrangements to photograph and record details of their quilts.

Almost all the owners of family quilts allowed me to bring their treasures to Auckland for the talented photographer of quilts, Anne Nicholas of Juzt Photos, to record their gems for the project. And in assisting me with filling out the documents these owners provided some amazing stories about their foremothers. As many of these people had already been working on their family genealogy, some were also able to supply photographs of the needlewomen.

I also made return visits to many of the major museums which I had earlier visited and when the staff saw the documents I was using, without fail every one of them commented that this is what they should have been doing themselves all along, and asked if they could have copies to use for their own records. As museums do not allow their collections off their premises, it was necessary for me to arrange with them to have their quilts professionally photographed, at my expense, and for them to fill out the documents. One exception to this, however, was

Reverse side of Sarah Armstong Wood's crazy patchwork quilt (seen on page 123), showing the central area with fabric samples and quilting.

Major Pitts of the Queen Elizabeth II Army Museum at Waiouru, who personally brought their splendid collection of signature quilts (see page 136 for more on signature quilts) to me one morning and waited in Auckland while I documented them and Anne dropped everything to take the photographs in time for the Major to collect the quilts a few days later. It all went with military precision — I hope the Major was pleased with our expertise.

Time and finances have not allowed me to revisit for this book all the museums I went to originally for the research project, but where a collection contains a quilt I needed to illustrate a particular point, I have in some instances been able to seek permission to include it and for the museum staff to rephotograph the item where I didn't have a suitable image. Occasionally in this book mention of a certain quilt in a collection is made, but no photograph is shown. If a reader is interested, it could be just the incentive they need to visit the museum in question, see just

what we have been lucky enough to preserve and so enjoy some of our feminine heritage.

To restrict the documenting to the category of old quilts, I decided to use the year 1950 as a cut-off point, thereby including any quilts that would have been made during the World War II years. As there had been little movement on the quilting scene in New Zealand after that date until well into the 1970s, and what was being made up until the beginning of the 1980s was not particularly innovative, I felt that the 1950s, 1960s and 1970s could be skipped. From approximately 1980 patchwork and quilting began to change so drastically that I felt that any further historical documentation could perhaps more appropriately start with the second half of the twentieth century. Much of the innovative work being done in the latter part of the twentieth century cannot be classed as bed quilting, for though many of these quilts are using updated versions of patchwork, they fall more into the category of fabric (or fibre) art wall hangings — outside the scope of this undertaking.

Over the years I have read assiduously about old quilts but I needed to do a certain amount of revision, as well as check and recheck many historical points. Exploring and documenting the very fabric of day-to-day lives inevitably provides a glimpse of earlier times, of history in the making. In my teens I benefited from the teachings of an excellent history teacher; recalling her early lessons brought home to me how social

This handsome quilt in the Broadgreen House collection, Stoke, is a splendid example of a sampler quilt, where each block is different, as are the borders. The maker's initials, CB, and the date, 1861, are in the centre of the quilt.

history can often have a significant bearing on the evolution of our rapidly changing lifestyles. In studying the old quilts I found a certain correlation between changes in the lives of the quilters and the quilts themselves. For those who think history is dull, perhaps they should forget about school lessons and the long lists of dates they had to memorise, and look at the subject from another perspective. The colourful old quilts which are part of our history certainly are not dull. If nothing else, I hope I have demonstrated in some way how much the early settler women contributed to the country's development and yet still found time to make quilts and leave us with a truly warm heritage to remember them by.

Patchwork and Quilting through the Ages

It has sometimes been inferred that women as great artists are such a rarity that those who have gained some modicum of fame in the visual arts are notable because they are women showing some success in a man's world, and not for the quality of their artistic ability. Lack of talent or genius may have justified this belief to a certain degree when reflecting on past painters and sculptresses, whose work seems to be virtually non-existent, though there must have been some creative feminine exponents of these art forms.

Even if these early women may not have coined the current slogan, our foremothers were quite aware that 'Women Can Do Anything', and because of their very nature surely must have tried their hands at various crafts. It is time, however, that this misconception of women not being great artists was refuted, for it is certainly not factual when considering the water-colourists and the beauty of work of, for instance, lacemakers and more especially needlewomen and what they achieved with their immense tapestries and fine embroideries. And then there are the homelier, more practically-based arts of patchwork and quilting.

These are spheres of creative handcraft where women of many countries reached heights of artistry in design, colour and craftsmanship that are quite breathtaking considering what was achieved with the most elementary ingredients, and in most cases little, if any, mathematical or artistic education. With the resurgence of quiltmaking in the United States that accompanied the patriotism engendered by the country's bicentenary celebrations in 1976, the hitherto humble crafts of patchwork and quilting finally gained official recognition as true art forms.

In some less developed countries various ethnic forms of patchwork and quilting in clothing and bedding are part of the ornamentation of necessities of life. In the western world, despite the availability of factory-made blankets, patchwork and quilting have never died out completely as crafts, or as a support in times of need. It is true, though, that in the main (apart from very low-income situations) they have usually enjoyed short bursts of interest more or less as hobbies rather than necessities in the provision of warm bedding.

The modern renaissance in quilting which has been sweeping the feminine world since the American bicentenary has inspired an interest in old quilts and their designs among a multitude of talented women (and some men) who are creating exciting new designs and using modern techniques. These folk are continuing the evolution of the quilt.

Through the ages the development of the quilt has, in many cases, been influenced by history, politics and sometimes superstition. To make a study of old quilts in one's own country it helps to know something of the evolution of quiltmaking, to more readily identify just where — in the vast universal 'patchwork quilt' — history has fitted in one's own little corner of the world.

Nobody really knows where or when quilting and patchwork originated, but history is filled with references that help us to trace their evolution. The earliest identified quilted item, now displayed in the British Museum, is seen on a small carved ivory figure of an Egyptian pharaoh of the First Dynasty (3400 BC) wearing what appears to be a quilted robe using a diamond pattern. In 1924 in a tomb excavated in Mongolia a quilted floor covering or carpet was discovered. It is believed to have been made between the first century BC and second century AD. It is intricately quilted and appliquéd with animals and trees by a truly expert and artistic needlewoman. The oldest piece of patchwork still in existence (a leather funeral pall) was made in Egypt some 3000 years ago.

Clothing wears out, and needs repair with patching. In time, to disguise the fact that it was a repair, the patching started to become an art form, culminating in the perfecting of the purely ornamental appliqué technique of needlework. This form of needlework is believed by some to be the true origin of patchwork.

Historians have long known that in the Middle East, ancient Greece, India and China, patchwork in various forms was being made centuries before the birth of Christ. To the dedicated contemporary patchworker it seems therefore quite obvious from the Old Testament Bible story of the coat of many colours that Israel made for his favourite son Joseph that this garment would most surely have been made from what we call pieced patchwork. 'Pieced' patchwork today means the 'piecing' together by the sewing of very small pieces of fabric to make a larger length of material. It is not patching as in mending.

Centuries later, in Europe, the colourful banners and flags of medieval knights were pieced together in a form of patchwork in all the bold primary colours of their heraldic designs. And in the East at this time, Saracens and Chinese wore quilted shirts under their armour as added protection from a slashing sword and to help overcome chafing by the metal edges of their armour. It is known that the Crusaders adopted the quilted protective shirts of their enemies, thereby possibly introducing quilting to Europe and England.

Historical paintings and illustrations record that the peasant classes of Europe seem to have used pieced patchwork for the making of bedding, and in Russia and other Asiatic countries people wore padded, quilted clothing for warmth. But little did anyone realise to what lengths skilled needlewomen would eventually extend and incorporate this 'new' idea into beautiful furnishings and clothing, or that it would become an important part of women's history.

Patchwork bed hangings, bedcovers, and quilts in particular have inspired women through the ages to create beautiful and intricate designs of colour and geometry, elegant appliqués, and subtle three-dimensional patterns in fine quilting. One has only to look at portraits of Queen Elizabeth I of England and her courtiers to see how important quilting had become in both male and female clothing. The royal courts set the standards for fashionable clothing which — minus the embellishments of gold and silver threadwork, pearls and precious stones — would be emulated by their subjects. Less luxurious fabrics may have been used, but the needlework could have been just as fine, for after all it was in many instances the subjects who would have sewn the garments of the lords and ladies.

Early examples of patchwork also include the Central Asian cashmere shawls that were originally woven of silk in small segments and then pieced together. As a point of interest, this is also an example of how one art form can lead to another. The beautiful cashmere shawls which were taken home to England by early sea captains as exotic and expensive gifts for their wives and sweethearts were greatly admired and coveted by other women. However, because it was virtually impossible to buy these desirable accessories to a lady's wardrobe, people of Paisley in Scotland copied the beautiful Eastern patterns and used them in the manufacture of the more affordable fine woollen Paisley shawls. The traditional beautiful cashmere designs are now known all over the world as the Paisley pattern, with virtually no recognition given to their origin. When it is used as a quilting motif, the design is referred to in Wales as Welsh pear, and in France as Kashmir cone, the latter giving acknowledgement to its origin.

When the English colonial settlers, the Puritan Pilgrims, went to America in 1620 the confined space of their ship, the tiny *Mayflower,* restricted the amount of cargo, and the amount of personal possessions each settler could take to the New World. The quilt, however, was one of the main items on the list of essentials, for not only was it used as a bedcover, but during the voyage it could also screen off a corner for privacy, or act as a warm shawl on deck. It was an important part of the furnishings for the new homes the settlers were to create, too, being repatched many times as parts wore out, and until time and material allowed for new quilts to be made. In crossing the Atlantic many things happened to the quilt, both in construction and in its involvement in the history of the 'new' country.

Traditional patchwork quilts involve two or three crafts:

Though patchwork is as old as the economic repairing of garments, the other two — piecing and quilting — are actually part of the evolution of the quilt.

2. Broderie Perse Appliqué: the process of sewing small pieces onto a larger piece is commonly known as appliqué, but frequently, and possibly more accurately, it is referred to as patchwork, as it resembles mending fabric by sewing a patch over a tear or worn part.

1. Patchwork and/or piecework: what in parts of the world is called patchwork — the making of a large sheet of fabric by sewing smaller pieces to one another — in America became known as piecework.

3. Quilting: quilting involves securing the layers of fabric (the top, the batting and the lining) with lines of stitches to prevent the batting from bunching up or 'migrating'. This also strengthens the construction seams. Some quilts are not actually quilted, but tied or tufted here and there at counterpoints to keep the three layers together.

The New World and its Quilts

American quilts, specifically the pieced and appliqué quilts, quite logically reflect the evolving history of the country. Many of the very early settlers perished from starvation, pneumonia or other diseases before their first winter in America was over. This was not only because of the lack of suitable shelter but also because they had set forth on their new venture quite unprepared and undersupplied for almost every hardship that beset them in the first years. Besides the limitation of cargo space, through ignorance and shortage of funds they lacked not only adequate food supplies and equipment, but also the tools to repair or replace what they had been able to take with them. What supplies they did have were barely sufficient to cover their own needs, let alone a surplus to barter with, and there were no shops from which to purchase the necessities of life — even if they could have afforded to buy goods.

By the middle of the seventeenth century, they also had to cope with the Navigation Acts, which were laws designed to protect England's trade monopolies, particularly in textiles. Among other frustrations, these laws made it illegal for colonists to buy textiles from any country but England, and a century later legislation in England made it illegal for them to export manufactured textiles themselves, even though the colonists were producing much of the raw cotton and wool for the English finished fabrics they were selling back to their colonies. Furthermore, it was illegal for anyone skilled in the textile trades to emigrate to America. This restriction covered not just spinners and weavers, but anyone who knew how to construct a spinning wheel or loom, or, more importantly, the more sophisticated machinery used in the textile industry. The English were not so concerned with coarse homespun, wool, linsey-woolsey and linen cloth for local consumption, as long as the secrets of producing fine printed cottons were protected.

The colonists had had to work out their own methods to dye their fabrics by using a whole range of different plants, and the instability of some of these dyes and lack of knowledge about printing the fabrics meant they posed little competition for old world manufacturers. However, by the time the colonists were able to produce fabric in excess to their own needs, the English were able to protect their own manufacturers by imposing an export ban. Bounties were paid to the colonies for the production of goods such as tobacco and indigo; but other items such as wool cloth were prohibited from export entirely. Equipment such as textile printing machinery was banned from export to the colonies. The French were also very strict in the keeping of their manufacturing secrets as there was great rivalry between Britain and France to protect all their export trades, including textiles.

Those women colonists who survived the many and various dangers involved in emigrating and the numerous challenging tasks involved in establishing a home found patchwork becoming an important part of their lives. Clothes were used until they wore out and fell apart, were cut down for the children and used again, and finally any usable scraps were sewn together to serve as bedding. Quilts were stuffed with whatever was found to give extra warmth — dried leaves, straw, corn husks, paper, or shreds of rags unsuitable for further piecing, patching or turning into rag floor-rugs.

Eventually, either the equipment needed to produce textiles was smuggled in or the settlers contrived to make suitable spinning wheels, looms, hoops and frames; and flocks of sheep were raised and linen flax was cultivated. Soon the Navigation Acts were simply being defied, and three colonies (for they were not yet independent states) passed their own laws requiring every woman, and child, to spin a certain amount of linen flax daily. Fleeces also became available for spinning and quilt batting. A few decades later, as cottons began to be exported to England and America by the (British) East India

Company, causing problems for the English wool and linen flax industries, England created more laws making it illegal in either England or the colonies to produce or import cotton. In 1729 it was even illegal to wear cotton. By 1736, due to the flagrant flouting of these laws, they were repealed. However, more new taxes were imposed on the unfortunate colonists, so that a length of fabric cost about four times what it did in England, and an additional tax was imposed on anyone using a spinning wheel or loom within their home. So tea, and its taxed importation from England, was only one of the many sources of irritation and growing anger that led to the 'Boston Tea Party' and the American Revolution (1775–83).

As annoying as these laws and taxes were, they also had a considerable effect on the value of even the scraps of fabrics available for quiltmaking. It would be some time before the 'new' American woman could afford to lose a few inches of her treasured hoard by cutting scraps and patches into shapes to create more attractive designs, let alone purchase fabric by the yard just for quilts, as most of us do today. When better times did come along, though, American women's artistic talents really blossomed, and following the Revolution, when the southern States began to establish their own cotton plantations, wool began to be replaced by cotton for the batting in quilts.

In both Europe and America it was quite customary in those days for families to sleep in one room. The younger children often shared their parents' bed or the beds of their siblings, who frequently slept on trundles, or truckles, stored by day under the high matrimonial bed. Consequently, quilts for this type of bed would often be made large enough to amply cover several bodies at night, and to cover the bed and conceal the trundles beneath by day. It was inconceivable that a woman would not make an abundance of bedding for her dowry and subsequently, after marriage, provide for her growing family. The skill of creating items of domestic and economic value with fabric, needle and thread was just as important as the ability to provide nourishing meals and carefully manage her other household duties. A well-trained and practical wife was a decided asset, and marriages at an early age were normal. Young men were always on the lookout for a hard-working potential mate; girls, in turn, trained virtually from babyhood, knew that they could make a good life through their marriage partner.

Traditionally at that time, all of a bride's real and personal property, as well as her bridal dowry, became her husband's possessions automatically with the taking of the marriage vows. As head of the family the husband dominated in thought, word and deed, and when he laid down the household rules women and children were expected to obey.

For the pilgrim and pioneer women of America, however, things began to change, for inevitably they became — had to become — partners of their men in a different sense from that prescribed by the customary matrimonial duties. Together they often had to toil for long tiring hours side by side to wrest the bare necessities of existence from the wilderness. Money was in short supply and its expenditure had to be carefully considered, so a barter system was very often the custom in many communities. If a bride was able to bring more than the customary dozen dowry quilts to her marriage this could prove a decided advantage, for a quilt surplus to needs could be used as a barter item in financially strained circumstances. Should there not be the need to make replacement quilts for her household, a diligent housewife could add to the family finances — as well as provide herself with a little nest egg — by taking in work to complete a patchwork top made by someone else not so adept at quilting.

Traditional masculine dominance was only one of the determinants of the control of family finances. The other was education. Even though the man of the house may have had a rudimentary education, he may not have had a shred of the practical shrewdness or intuition of his wife, who frequently would have no book learning. However, being of the 'educated class' he was expected to have sound judgement, and so would keep up the bluff. In families where comparative wealth might provide an easier and more cultured existence there could still be many restrictions to deny women the expression of their own individuality in the decoration of their homes and often even in the selection of their gowns, for the husband still held the purse strings.

It was in their needlework, however, that American women could now freely demonstrate their artistic talents. Servants and slaves might have allowed for a more leisurely way of life, but idleness was still considered to be a deadly sin. The mistress, daughters and other female relatives who frequently might have made up the extended family therefore plied their needles all the more diligently and became highly skilled in both plain sewing and all kinds of embroidery. They were still expected to supply many of the household necessities, and the quilt was practical, essential to comfort, and an excellent medium for teaching daughters needlework skills. As this was within the economic means of the household's daily expenses, sewing skills would also be taught to servants and slaves, who would have mending and darning as part of their duties.

In America examples still exist of the fine quilts created by adept Black women under the guidance of their mistresses. Also found have been examples of warm and colourful quilts with design motifs made by these women seeking to express their own culture using scraps left from making quilts for their owners' household. Though they endeavoured to copy the 'big house' quilts, lack of measuring tools meant that

some of the geometrics might appear somewhat eccentric. However, they reveal a charm of their own, and though a number of their appliqué quilts tried to illustrate Bible stories, those referring to their own life stories are of more historical significance.

Prior to the abolition of slavery, runaway slaves knew they could find safe houses for a brief respite through a system of patchwork quilts hung on a clothesline or the balustrade of a porch, somewhat in the manner that gypsies leave secret messages for their tribes to follow. The slaves would then be passed along this network in what became known as the 'underground railway', on their flight northwards towards freedom. Thus in later years some quilt designs were given the name Underground Railway or something similar. There are many Black women included in the ranks of the current quilting renaissance who fully appreciate the fact that they have their place in the evolution of quiltmaking.

As the pioneers pushed back the frontiers and ventured deeper into the wilderness of the vast continent, the quilt went too, continuing to fulfil the needs of women to create something beautiful yet practical. However, not content with the old traditional English patterns, they evolved an ever-increasing number of complex designs, finding their inspiration in not only the everyday tools and household equipment, but also the new flowers, trees, birds and animals they were discovering along the way. Indian designs were also adapted for inclusion in these new patterns. And just as their creators travelled, so did the designs, as they were passed on to friends and relatives in other parts of the country. In being passed on the patterns sometimes were renamed, so a certain design could end up having half a dozen or more fancy names. Inevitably some of the new designs also found their way to Canadian settler friends and back to England.

With the new designs and names there also evolved fanciful identities and superstitions. Wandering Foot, for example, had its name changed to Turkey Tracks in an attempt to lift what some considered a curse on this beautiful design. It would be thought very rash to allow a child to sleep under a quilt with such a risky name, as it was feared that malevolent forces associated with such a name could foster a tendency towards discontent and instability. It would be bad enough for little girls to develop an 'unfeminine' roving disposition, but young boys, already more adventurous by nature, might be led to all manner of disasters — even fatalities — in a wild, untamed frontier still heavily forested and possibly harbouring venomous snakes and wild animals. Young men who had survived to adulthood were also at risk in case they responded to the lure of the gold rush into the West, as hundreds of them in fact did, and were never heard from again. To have a son or brother who had gone West (in search of the elusive

gold) soon acquired the sadder meaning which that phrase still has today when we use the colloquialism that someone has 'gone West' meaning the person has died. No bride-to-be would be foolish enough to risk losing her betrothed by including a Wandering Foot quilt in her dowry chest. So the practical pioneer women, rather than abandon such an attractive pattern, simply changed the name to Turkey Tracks.

It was also considered bad luck for a girl to use images of hearts, wedding rings or lovers' knots when making her dowry quilts. Incorporating such elements would risk the fate of being left on the shelf in the same manner as a prematurely created bridal quilt may. Only when a betrothal was announced could the bridal quilt be made that included those special emblems; by this time the bride-to-be would also be an expert needlewoman, able to create a quilt of real beauty worthy of this momentous event in her life.

Often, if there were many daughters in a family there could be limited storage space in the house, so the dowry quilts would not be completed until a betrothal was announced, whereupon large social quilting bees of friends and family were held to quilt the tops. The bridal quilt, however, was customarily made by the bride or her mother.

In strict religious communities, such as the Amish (whose quilts are so beautiful in their simple designs of plain coloured fabrics and exquisite quilting) it was customary for the quilters to make a deliberate error in their work. Within their humble, rigidly pious way of life it was considered that only God could make anything perfect. So in case they were presumed by their families or church elders to have tried to outdo God the quilters would, for example, deliberately include an unmatched piece of material or place a block sideways or upside down. By making such 'mistakes' they would not be tempted to stray from their paths of virtue.

Incorporating significant elements in quilts was also a way of recording history and quilts frequently featured picture appliqués, design titles or the adventures some quilters were a party to. Though there is no solid evidence for it, the first American flag is said to have been made by a seamstress named Betsy Ross using the pieced patchwork technique. During wartime, quilts frequently played a direct part in history, often being put to very practical use. They were a means of smuggling medicines, maps and secret papers; a quilt may have protected a child during Indian raids, or covered the bed of a war hero, visiting politician, or even a president, and some quilt block designs were given the names of political slogans.

In more peaceful times, quilts also had additional uses. When one was travelling, small treasures, especially jewellery, could be hidden for safe keeping within the batting of a quilt, a custom probably brought with the settlers when they crossed the Atlantic. While searching out old quilts in New Zealand, I came across a woman who told me about a quilt her husband's grandmother had sent him. Several years after receiving it, when she was showing the quilt to a friend, a hard lump was found near one edge. Upon carefully unpicking this patch they discovered a diamond brooch which the grandmother had either forgotten she had hidden there or had omitted to tell them about.

When young men left home to seek fame and fortune it was the custom to present them with a Freedom quilt. Many of the thousands of men who left their homes to fight in the Civil War were given a quilt to use as a bedroll, an important part of their survival equipment, which all too often might have ended up becoming their shroud.

The recording of American history in quilts still continues today. The Watergate quilt was stitched while the creator watched on TV the various stages of that momentous trial involving a Republican break-in to Democrat headquarters by presidential officials during the 1972 elections. Hundreds of bicentenary quilts were made in the mid-1970s, and later hundreds more to celebrate the hundredth birthday of the Statue of Liberty. A Yellow Ribbons quilt was made by a patriotic woman to celebrate the release of the group of American hostages who had been held captive by the Iranians when Ayatollah Khomeini came to power. Doubtless many other quilts were made to commemorate the brief Desert Storm war, in 1991, but a hitherto-unthought-of step in the evolution of quiltmaking also occurred during that war. Women (other than nurses) were included in the fighting forces and some of them actually took pieces of patchwork with them to work on during the breaks in their duties.

Brought about by the grimness of life in the very earliest American settlements, quilting later became a regular part of the social calendar, with quilting bees in both town and country becoming one of the most popular forms of feminine social functions. As soon as the winter snows thawed and country roads, lanes and tracks became passable and safer for travelling, women would emerge from their isolation and gather to quilt the tops they had pieced while housebound by inclement weather. And as they quilted together they exchanged new recipes, patterns, the latest news and gossip. Sometimes a quilting bee would be held to coincide with gatherings of their men helping a farmer raise a new barn or bring in the harvest. After the day's work was completed the evening would be devoted to more pleasurable activities, and inevitably political discussions would develop, so women were always familiar with important events and might record them by naming new patchwork designs after them.

Sometimes in the harsh and frequently uncomfortable pioneering days spare quilts would be fastened to the walls of a log cabin to provide colourful insulation from the wintry draughts which relentlessly whistled through roughly-constructed walls. When in more recent decades the United States was struck with a fuel crisis, some modern-day quilters found inspiration in this proven pioneer strategy and began making window quilts to help prevent heat loss through the large expanses of glass in modern homes, thus minimising escalating fuel costs. After a disaster such as a tornado, flood or house fire it was customary in earlier times for friends and neighbours to rally around to help the victims. Damaged properties were thus repaired or rebuilt, and essential items replaced from neighbours' own supplies, including quilts. This custom prevails today with the Mennonite people in particular when, after a state or national disaster either in Canada or the United States, they quietly arrive with supplies and quilts and, after assisting to repair the damage, just as quietly leave. Of course such direct aid in times of need was not confined to the Mennonites. It was part of the Christian teachings of the settlers to help one another, though it could be days before news filtered through to alert them to any difficulties nearby. Nowadays, when terrible disasters strike anywhere on the globe, modern communication systems flash the news to all corners of the world, and people of all nationalities and creeds rush to help. And quilters are usually among the most generous of the good

Previous page: A beautiful Victorian Log Cabin quilt (detail right) from the collection of the Museum of Transport and Technology, Auckland. There are 60 blocks measuring 4″ x 4″ surrounding a central medallion square. Each block has a central square on point with rows of strips surrounding it. All manner of luxurious richly coloured fabrics have been used and many squares have been beaded, sequined and/or gold braided, the larger central block being the most ornately decorated. It has a large central pearl in the middle of a beaded and sequined star. The cream lace border has scallop shapes with a point at the middle edge of the scallop. There is an unknown natural fibre batting but no quilting. The quilt is lined with cream linen. 24″ x 40″, plus lace. Maker unknown.

Samaritans. They not only provide quilts for those in need but also replace fabrics, 'tools of the trade' and all the paraphernalia required by the modern quilter.

Quilting is a form of therapy for many quilters and they may experience withdrawal symptoms if unable to continue with what is often a large part of their life.

The Freedom quilts, made earlier for young men upon gaining their majority, when they frequently left home to seek fame and fortune, have their parallel today in the quilts that young people of both sexes take with them when they leave home to study or work in another city or state. When a friend is moving to another part of the country, or world, Friendship quilts are still made by groups of women as a parting gift, and quilting bees remain a popular form of fundraising for a favourite charity or community project.

With the advent of the sewing machine around 1846 those wealthy enough to acquire one of these wonderful pieces of equipment naturally began to use them to make their quilts, though purists decry this method. In their collection of antique quilts the Smithsonian Institute in Washington D.C. have two quilts which give a wonderful example of this controversial subject of whether a quilt should be entirely hand-stitched or made quickly using a sewing machine. One beautiful quilt was lovingly hand-stitched by a young woman for her first-born child, and doubtless has stitched into it all her hopes and dreams for the expected baby. The other was made by her husband; after chiding her for the long hours 'wasted' in creating her elegant masterpiece, he emphasised the point by sewing on the machine, in a fraction of the time his devoted wife had taken, an equally beautiful quilt. There, in perfect condition in one of the temperature-controlled storerooms of the institute, the two quilts hang side by side, a mute demonstration of an argument that continues today. Asked to select which is the more beautiful, though each quilt seems to call 'choose me, choose me', who could determine such a thing? I couldn't, for they are both lovely.

A wonderful example of the desire to create something beautiful for a special baby can be seen in New Zealand in the collection of quilts at Auckland's Museum of Transport and Technology (MOTAT). On pages 24–25 is an opulent Log Cabin (see page 46 for more on the Log Cabin technique) variation crib quilt, rich in all the luxurious fabrics and embellishments beloved of the Victorian era. The unknown needlewoman most certainly did her baby proud.

As well as speeding up the process, the sewing machine brought about changes in quilting techniques. Seminole patchwork, for example — a form of strip-piecing patchwork — was invented by the Seminole Indians of the Florida region only after the sewing machine became available to them. This colourful style provides a quick method of making exciting geometric strips of squares or oblongs which can be manipulated into numerous patterns, sometimes with the squares slanting, or forming simple stylised flowers. These patchwork strips were used mainly to decorate clothing but the technique

was quickly adopted by the rest of the quilting world as part of the patchwork repertoire, and to extend the technique into creating other forms of strip piecing.

Though patchwork and quilting fell out of favour in many parts of the world, pockets of quilters continued to work away at their craft. In the 1920s and 1930s in the United States it remained a popular and sometimes financially rewarding pastime, ably supported by periodicals and newspapers which regularly featured articles and new patterns and often provided a mail order service for either patterns or whole kitsets which included the fabrics.

During the years of the Great Depression in the 1930s, of necessity in many instances, patchwork and quilting once again grew in popularity for some quilters. They may not have been paid more than a pittance for a finished quilt, or for quilting someone else's patchwork top, but the few dollars they did earn were often enough to literally keep them from starving. Some experienced quilters became household icons via their regular newspaper columns, and their names have become part of the history of American quilting. In 1934 the American manufacturers of quilt batting, Stearns & Foster Company, did a survey which revealed, in their estimation, that more than 400 metropolitan newspapers regularly printed information or a column on patchwork and quilting. One of the women who had a syndicated newspaper column was

Ruby Short McKim, who, prior to 1920, had been sharing her embroidery skills for designing embroidered blocks, and in 1929 began to turn her talents to designing patchwork blocks. In 1931 the McKim Studios published her book *101 Patchwork Patterns,* which quickly became the most popular reference book for the large sisterhood of patch-workers. Dover Publications published a revised version of this book in 1962.

In 1933 Chicago hosted a World's Fair and, as one of the events to entice people to their exhibition hall, American mail-order giant Sears, Roebuck & Company set quilters alight by announcing a contest with a tantalising US$7,500 in prizes. The contest was run through a series of heats with varying amounts of prize money gradually increasing as the selected quilts passed through the stages. The top 30 quilts which reached the ten regional semifinals went through for the final judging with the winner receiving US$1,200 (an amalgamation of the various regional prizes, step by step, and the final grand prize). In those days this prize equated in value to well over the cost of a large luxury car. It was no wonder that about 15,000 women entered the contest.

Quilting in Other Parts of the World

While all this development in patchwork and quilting was occurring in America, over the centuries people in other parts of the world were creating or extending their own styles.

In Vietnam, the Hmong people were busily sewing their particular version of fine reverse appliqué, and the women of the San Blas Islands in the Panama area were creating their distinctive Molas using a more primitive form of reverse appliqué. In both countries this needlework was used mainly as a decorative part of their clothing. As soon as the American missionaries began their evangelical work amongst the Pacific Island groups the wives of these churchmen were quick off the mark to teach the local women how to sew; first garments to cover up their nudity and then domestic items, and in particular quilts.

In Hawaii, a new form of appliqué and quilting evolved. Initially a large square of plain bright cotton was folded several times, then a design was cut out, frequently in the form of a flower and/or leaf, in the same way school children cut snowflake patterns out of folded squares of paper. The pattern revealed on unfolding displays a motif, repeated fourfold, one in each corner (or more, depending on how many times the original square has been folded). When adapted to large folded squares of plain fabric, even a simple motif can be disclosed, on unfolding the material, as a surprisingly more complicated design. The quilters basted their cut-out fabric pattern onto a larger square of contrasting coloured cotton, appliquéd it in place and quilted the layered top with row upon row of stitching following the contoured outlines of the design. As there was not the need in their climate for the bed covers to provide a lot of warmth, batting was not usually used, which meant the stitching became very fine.

In Samoa and Rarotonga, yet another form of this appliqué was evolving — the tivaevae. Similar in many ways to the Hawaiian quilts, this version attaches the appliqués with embroidered stitches, which are also used for surface details. When variegated coloured embroidery cottons or silks became available these incorporated extra embellishment into the colourful tivaevae. However, as a change from the appliquéd tivaevae, some of these bedcovers use designs created with small squares of fabric pieced together, giving the appearance of

A Log Cabin variation in the exuberant colours of the Pacific, from the collection of the Whakatane District Museum and Gallery.

mosaic tiling. The overall effect of the tivaevae is an exuberant display of bright, colourful flowers, a reflection of what the needlewomen see in the lush flora of their surroundings.

In Britain, the homes of the aristocracy and wealthy always included quilts as part of their furnishings. Though the servants could rarely aspire to such luxury for themselves or their families they certainly knew how to make quilts; part of their duties may have required them to help make them. In the late seventeenth century, by law, it was still required that inventories of deceased adults' possessions be made along with their wills, and existing records always include quilts. Such inventories made later in America also included quilts. Old records of clearance sales of properties in both countries frequently list quilts, sometimes in great detail.

Many famous women are known to have made quilts. Rumour had it that Mary Queen of Scots made a quilt while in captivity before she was executed, but this has been refuted by some. She was, however, an extremely skilled and talented needlewoman, having been tutored in this art form as part of her childhood education when living in exile in France and did in fact occupy much of her time working on her embroideries. Most quilters know that Ann Hathaway, in her will, bequeathed her second-best quilt to her husband, William Shakespeare. In fact this quilt might have been in far better fettle than the 'best' one. Though possibly made from superior fabrics and with much better needlework, the 'best' quilt may also have been used much more, for it would doubtless have been placed on the bed provided for visitors. The one left to William may possibly have had a lot less wear and tear. Eighteenth-century novelist Jane Austen also made quilts, for it was probably a requirement for the young ladies of her era to be able to make quilts to form part of their dowry.

In the more modest homes and cottages in the British Isles a quilt may have taken pride of place in the best bedroom. Only in the latter part of the eighteenth century — when they had begun to go out of fashion with the upper classes — did quilts come into favour with the lower classes as they became more affordable. Farmers' wives and daughters and cottage dwellers also found that making domestic quilts was an additional way of supplementing their meagre incomes. With the industrial revolution cotton fabrics came within their price range and though the country women may not have had ready access to a retail shop, there were frequent visits from travelling pedlars carrying a large range of printed cottons. From these the quilters could select their requirements to create the medallion quilts which had become so popular. Though little seems to have changed in either techniques or designs, the medallion and beautiful whole-cloth quilts were still being made in the mid-seventeenth and well into the eighteenth centuries, with the latter sometimes including the extra refinement of cording and stuffing (trapunto) which had gained in popularity.

Trapunto (a technique that involves stuffing) had been used in Sicilian quilt designs since at least the thirteenth century, and was also the main style used in Provence (France). Once these quilts appeared in England, many English quilters had a source of new designs to incorporate into their elaborate and intricate whole-cloth quilting designs.

The addition of padding and cording gave their quilts a greater three-dimensional appearance. This form of quilting was also used in beautiful quilted garments, in particular the elegant silk petticoats favoured by highborn ladies of France, a style quickly adopted by fashionable English ladies around the time

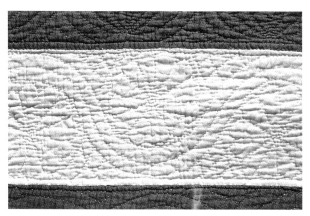

Detail from a quilt by Sarah Pridhoe North (page 126) showing intricate 'Cable and Flower' quilting.

that the fleeing Huguenots arrived in their midst.

Though quilting designs were used for garments the cording and stuffing usually were not. The new fashionable gowns worn over the quilted petticoats, however, were open down the front to reveal a separate bodice and the very elegant petticoat below the split-front skirt. (New Zealand's Canterbury Museum has a collection of some of these beautiful petticoats.) With so many women wanting to be fashionable those of lesser means began quilting their cotton petticoats but often just looped, or tucked up, the overskirt to show off their version of the fashionable petticoat.

The intricate whole-cloth quilting was used not only for gentlemen's vests and jackets, women's bodices, jackets and skirts, but also for beautiful quilts and bed hangings. Such was the demand in France for this quilting that many ateliers (similar to lacemakers' establishments) were set up employing young girls

and women of all ages to turn out as much work as possible, not only for the local trade but also for export. As many of these establishments were in the south of France, especially around Marseilles, this type of work became known as broderie de Marseilles. When fashionable American ladies adopted the dress style they also adopted the cording and trapunto techniques into their quilting.

By 1763 demand was out-pacing production both in France and in England, so two enterprising Englishmen, Robert Elder and George Glascow, invented a special loom for weaving a fabric that would look somewhat like the Marseilles quilting. It did not look quite as good, as the bedcovers made from it did not require lining, batting or time-consuming quilting. Nonetheless this fabric remained popular for lightweight bedcovers well into the twentieth century and the sturdy white counterpanes were a customary part of many homes the world over.

In New Zealand there was hardly a home that wasn't furnished with Marsella counterpanes, as they came to be called. For many years virtually every hospital bed in the country was topped with the snowy white Marsellas. They were sturdy enough to tolerate frequent boilings in both household and hospital coppers; there were no colours to fade; and they were able to withstand harsh southern hemisphere sunlight when hung out to dry after laundering. After they began to wear out they were often relegated to being used as 'under-blankets' between the mattress and the supporting wire-wove base of the bed. In New Zealand these bedspreads gradually disappeared from the shop shelves during the late 1930s and 1940s, perhaps because fashions change or possibly because the English and European factories, if still operating, were busy manufacturing more essential items of need in the austere years of World War II. However, 'What goes round comes round': lo and behold, with the coming of the year 2000 several shops in New Zealand were advertising Marsella bedspreads — one of them Marsella bedspreads from Portugal. But these days, when items become a fashion statement either for interior decorating in the home or exterior decoration of the human form, they seem to be exceptionally expensive. So it is with these 'new' covers: they cost comparatively much more than the colonial woman would have expected to pay for her standard counterpanes.

With the Victorian era came the next innovation: the elaborate 'crazy' patchwork quilt. Prim Victorian ladies were not supposed to show an ankle, let alone a leg, so the lower limbs were amply covered by voluminous pantaloons and layers of petticoats which by this time were made of snowy white cambric or cotton with flannel petticoats being added for winter warmth. There was not a sign of the elaborate quilted garments of yore, let alone a glimpse of what was hidden within their folds. Some women took this

fashion to the extreme and a fad developed for covering furniture with draperies. These coverings were often 'crazy' patchwork, as were the chair and sofa cushions. Mantelpieces and shelves were also covered and the former, in particular, often sported fine examples of richly coloured patchworks with lots of stuffed motifs, such as birds, flowers, grapes, berries, and an assortment of other fruits.

Examples of these patchworks can often be seen in some of the smaller museums in New Zealand. Crazy patchwork quilts, or throws (a small quilt draped effectively across the end of a chaise longue or sofa ready to be brought into use when 'milady' decided to take a little rest), were made from odd-shaped scraps of velvets, silks, satins, brocades, ribbons and so on. The makers were then able to demonstrate their repertoire of embroidery stitches to conceal the seams and in many instances to create small pictures on some of the larger scraps. Sometimes they embroidered their signatures and significant dates. Less wealthy needlewomen, who could not aspire to create such a luxurious quilt, used scraps of bright and pretty cottons, and more often than not the only extra embellishment would be the covering of the seams with feather stitching in a contrasting colour.

The intricately quilted whole-cloth quilts never went out of fashion, especially those from Durham, Cumbria, Northumbria and Wales, and the traditional quilters of these (apart from the women of

Provence) are still the best exponents of this style of quilting. However, the emergence of factory-made Marsella quilts, poor copies of the old French Marseilles quilts, did have quite a drastic effect upon the popularity of the beautiful and painstakingly handmade whole-cloth quilt. It was much cheaper for customers to pick-up a look-alike bedcover that had been mass produced using a Jacquard-style loom.

Overall, the industrial era had a dramatic impact on traditional communities in the United Kingdom. By the end of the nineteenth century many country folk had already migrated to the cities, seeking work, and the more adventurous even decided to emigrate to Canada, the United States, Australia or New Zealand, many of the women taking their quilts and needlework skills with them.

The Emergence of New Zealand Patchwork and Quilting

Maritime explorers from several European countries claimed to have been the first white men to discover New Zealand, but Dutch explorer Abel Tasman is generally credited with a greater claim to this honour. In 1642, while Tasman was in the service of the Dutch East India Company as a ship's skipper, the company's governor, Antonio Van Diemen, despatched him from Batavia (Jakarta) on an exploratory venture to the southern Pacific. Tasman did discover a new land, but did not claim the land for his country, nor come ashore. (With subsequent explorations the Dutch name Nieuw Zeeland eventually became New Zealand.)

English and French ships too had been fleetingly visiting New Zealand, but it wasn't until 1769–70

that the English navigator Captain James Cook took possession of the country for his king (George III).

Other sailing ships also made stopovers, firstly seeking timber to replace damaged masts and spars, then later to trade. Sealers and whalers, however, from the late eighteenth century, were the first white men to settle in New Zealand for any length of time. They formed tiny coastal bases, many men taking Maori women for their wives. And as the small settlements began to grow, they became very dangerous and lawless places, so the next white people to arrive, around 1814, were English and French missionaries.

From that time, and for the rest of the nineteenth century, adventurous settlers arrived in greater and greater numbers, mostly from the British Isles but some from Denmark, Norway, Switzerland and, later, Yugoslavia. After the discovery of gold, however, in the mid-nineteenth century, fortune hunters came from many more countries.

In 1861 Charles Hursthouse, who had made several journeys to New Zealand, partly on fact-finding excursions before finally settling in Taranaki, published a book — *New Zealand the 'Britain of the*

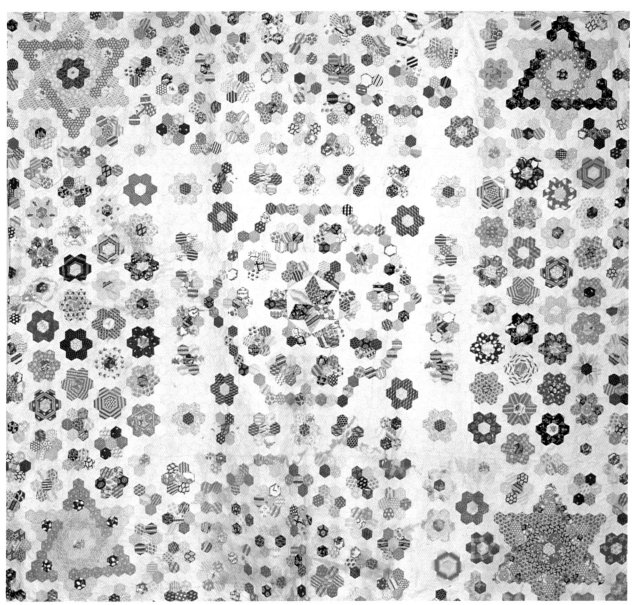

Little is known about this coverlet in the collection of Broadgreen House, Nelson. It is believed to have been sewn circa 1830–1875 and is 81" wide by 78¾" long. Hexagons and diamonds have been used in an interesting way to create a medallion in the centre, and flowers and stars — a very original design.

South' — which provided prospective settlers with a huge wealth of information, including what to bring with them to set up their homes. The lists of recommended items related to all social and economic levels of prospective settlers, as regards farming equipment, tools of trade, kitchen equipment, furniture, linens, and clothing. Hursthouse's book also advised on how the class system worked on board ship, as well as how much equipment could be transported as part of the fare, and how to pack it. For instance, if you were wealthy and could afford cabin class you didn't just walk onto the ship and into a well fitted-out cabin. Upon booking and paying for your voyage you were allocated a certain amount of deck space on which you had to have your cabin built, so Hursthouse listed reputable firms who undertook this work. He also advised how the cabin should be finished and furnished to make good use of the space so that the fittings and so on could be dismantled and taken ashore to become part of the home to be set up upon arrival.

The class of passage paid for also governed the amount of cargo space allocated so Hursthouse also advised on the style of crating or packaging. For example, he advised using barrels for transporting chinaware, which should be wrapped in small textile items as added protection against breakage; as further protection the spaces around these treasures should be filled with grass seed, which would later be a valuable item for the farmers in particular. Upon disembarkation, after the unpacking was done, the barrels were to serve as pickling or rain barrels, or could be cut in half and used as tubs for washing dishes, clothes or dairy accessories.

Of particular interest is the fact that although Hursthouse detailed household linens, curtains, carpet, etc., and feather beds, he made no mention of quilts. He did advise, however, not to sell up everything before embarkation with the idea of purchasing the necessities of the home upon arrival, as this would be impossible. Even though there were already quite a number of established and growing settlements, shipments of goods for sale were snapped up almost as soon as they were unloaded from the trading vessels.

Prospective settlers of lesser means were allocated minimum space on the lower decks (not cabin space) and the only privacy available was within the confines of the allocated bunks. The remainder of the accommodation area on the deck was used for communal living, including cooking and dining. The less well off you were, the less space you had and the less space there was within the holds for your personal effects and any furnishings and work equipment you were able to bring with you. Whichever socio-economic class you belonged to, you would need a great deal of forward planning before venturing to leave your motherland, and that is why Mr Hursthouse advised not to sell up everything, but to judiciously select what best to bring.

Many women, aware that they would be months at sea (sometimes almost half a year), had the forethought to provide themselves with well-stocked needlework baskets to help occupy their time, as well as make something of use and/or beauty to add to their wardrobe or household soft goods. A number of quilts still around today were made by early settlers during the voyage out. Many a woman saddened by leaving her family and friends, probably never to see them again, must have gained some solace from sewing her patchwork, and when she used pieces of fabric given to her by those women dear to her whom she had left behind, her quilt probably became a real memory quilt. She would only need to look at certain pieces to conjure up the happy or momentous occasions upon which a special friend or sister wore the dress from which the scraps had come.

However, by the time these emigrants began to leave England, factory-made blankets would have been readily available and very reasonably priced. A fair number of settlers must have brought these blankets with them, or they wouldn't have been used as a barter item to trade with Maori (as records show). Nonetheless, many quilts could have crossed the seas as part of the bedding the travellers on lower-priced fares had to provide for themselves. These lower-

priced fares, including steerage, required travellers to cook their own meals from the meagre supplies provided by the shipping company, as well as provide their own eating utensils and bedding. Some of the women on the lower decks were also able to augment the money they brought with them by undertaking to do the cooking for their deckmates, especially since a fair proportion of their shipmates would have been young men seeking to make their fortunes in the newly established colony.

One possible reason for Mr Hursthouse's book not mentioning quilts may have been that he felt they were such a common part of the household effects and would be included as a matter of course. If they were indeed included, the more probable reason why many more have not survived would be that they were used over and over, or relegated to under-blanket status between mattress and wire-wove base of a bed before finally being dumped by later generations. Most certainly many quilts would not have survived the rigours of frequent laundering and then being hung out to dry under the very destructive strong rays of the New Zealand sunshine. The use of candles for lighting and some fairly dangerous means of cooking meals in settler cottages or whares also increased the frequency of house fires, and quilts would most certainly have been fuel to such a disaster.

Besides clergy, a handful of professional men, and men hopeful of making a fortune through land speculation, the early male settlers were mainly farmers and timber workers. The latter were needed to help clear the forests for the farmers and to provide timber for building, and along with these two trades the blacksmiths, wheelwrights, and carpentry tradesmen were in great demand. Other newcomers were army personnel brought out to help protect the settlers, small businessmen and traders interested in catering to the needs of the growing settlements, and both men and women labourers and domestic helpers, whose services were greatly sought after.

Some families did bring quilts with them, and some women did work on their patchwork quilts on the long, often dangerous journey. But the toil involved in setting up a home and eking out an existence in the new colony does not appear to have provided women with enough leisure time for making quilts, other than simple utilitarian ones to add to or replace worn out bedcovers. The women naturally stayed with designs familiar to them rather than spend what leisure hours they may have had in developing new patterns. Besides the usual housework and cooking, they needed to establish vegetable gardens and orchards, preserve any resultant produce when there was any to spare, perhaps milk the house-cow and make butter, and also make the daily loaves of bread, and in many instances their own candles, too.

They also sewed clothes for the whole family; hemmed household linen; and taught their daughters to do plain sewing, make embroidered samplers, and knit, tat and crochet; but rarely do letters home mention sewing their patchwork and they certainly do not mention gathering for quilting bee parties. Many of these women had been accustomed to having household maids and possibly even a cook, and were thrust into an abrupt learning exercise of having to do so many unaccustomed tasks for themselves and their families.

Nevertheless, some of these women were still making patchwork bedcovers using the traditional English paper method in particular, and whether it was because they were not skilled in quilting, or there was a lack of something to use for the batting, many left the papers inside the scrap pieces. Frequently the patchwork bedcovers were unlined, which could indicate a lack of funds, fabric supplies, or time to add the finishing touches. Together with other old lined quilts where the papers may become visible through a tear or a worn-out segment, the papers left in place in these unlined bedcovers have been a godsend: they often reveal a date on an old letter or document.

Most of the early settler patchworkers stayed with their tried and trusted hexagons, diamonds, squares, octagons and what we now refer to as Log Cabins, though in the main they did not know that name, given by the Americans to a design long used by their foremothers. Many used shirt materials for their

A selection of popular quilting styles. Opposite is a detail from Euphemia Maxwell's wonderful Crazy Quilt (see page 116). Below left are hexagons, used here to create a traditional 'Flower Garden' pattern (see page 54), and below right the ancient Log Cabin quilting style (see page 46). At left is a less common design using long hexagons (sometimes called 'Church Windows' or 'Coffins') and squares to form octagons. The central octagon is hand-painted.

scraps, which could indicate that they may have had some connection with a large English cotton mill, either as an ex-employee or through a family member working there. The wide variety of printed cottons that they used suggests some such connection along the way, or a tremendous amount of swapping of fabrics amongst those who were still quietly sewing their patchwork. Others could have been dressmakers and thus they, and the more affluent of the colonial women who employed them, appear to have been the ones with access to better quality fabrics. The latter would also have had the hours and wherewithal to make the more time-consuming appliqués, embroidered and crazy patchworks. They and their dressmakers and tailors had the availability of not only the better quality cottons and linens but also the more luxurious fabrics, such as the brocades, chintzes, grosgrain, satins, taffetas and velvets.

With the turn of the century, daily existence gradually became less harsh, bringing a progressively changing lifestyle. Women still knew about patchwork and quilting though they rarely practised this form of needlework. There is evidence that in times of need some were making patchwork bedcovers, especially during the Depression years of the 1930s. Several older owners of old quilts who volunteered their quilts for the research programme indicated that their grandmothers or mothers always had patchwork bedcovers on all their beds.

During both World Wars I and II, signature quilts were being made as fundraisers to provide money to purchase comforts for the troops serving overseas. Squares of white calico, cotton or linen were used for these quilts, the better to show up the embroidered signatures. During World War II, when we in New Zealand were living in a state of relative austerity, some patchworkers started to revive the old craft. Shortages prescribed a make do and mend approach, but the quilt revival was also begun to provide for those in need, whether across the other side of the world or in New Zealand. As one woman revealed, she had been a young married mother with two children and needed bedcovers for them. She made two Log Cabins and tried to copy a patchwork quilt which had belonged to her late mother-in-law — though she was too late to copy it exactly, as the old quilt had gone to the tip with other items of no use to anyone after the old lady's death. Only 45 years later, when patchwork took off again as a wonderful pastime, did this person find out the name of this old style of design.

European women in New Zealand have always been avid and diligent needlewomen. Little evidence has been found, however, of Maori women making quilts. Until missionary wives and nuns arrived they knew little of sewing, but these pioneers soon taught Maori girls how to wield a needle, firstly to help them make clothing, but also to provide them with the

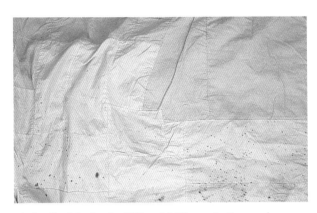

A detail of the back of Elisa McPherson's diamond pattern quilt (see page 66). Her quilt had no batting or quilting and was lined with flour bags, a very practical response to the materials available at the time.

means of earning a living. Maori women may not have felt the need to make a quilt when they could barter for a blanket, but if they became passably adept at sewing this was an extra talent to add to their domestic abilities which could gain them employment in the homes of wealthier settlers. However, in the 1970s, there was an elderly Maori woman living at Ruatahuna who knew how to make utility quilts. She had one which she called a paparua, made from old tweed jackets, skirts and coats, and though it was not a thing of traditional beauty it had been crafted with a lot of love as a warm and very efficient bed-covering for a grandson who had been in her care.

As a nation New Zealanders have always been inveterate do-it-yourself exponents in the daily maintenance of every aspect of our living and quick to adopt new fashions and styles, whether it be painting

the house, making curtains, sewing or knitting the family's clothes, or making a kite, a trolley or a model aeroplane. Quilts started to become less common as, true to form, new fashions and styles were adopted. In their turn, quilts eventually gave way to blankets and eiderdowns (often referred to as quilts in the early days), and then to electric blankets and duvets (surely an eiderdown by another name).

We have also been great throwers away. One such 'reject' found in the course of research for this book seems to have once been a handsome medallion coverlet with broderie perse appliqués using parts of a palampore (printed bedcover originally imported to England from India) in its central square and corner blocks, and surrounded with plain and scalloped pieced borders. It had been retrieved from a rubbish tip and donated to the small museum at Te Aroha. This bedcover had been made in England, possibly around the turn of the eighteenth century or the early years of the nineteenth, but the deterioration of the fabrics is such that various parts of the prints have disappeared completely, leaving just the outline of what may have been part of a paisley or leaf pattern or some other motif.

Between 1820 and 1856 dye masters had begun using various harsh minerals and metals as mordants to stabilise the customary natural dyes used by the textile manufacturers in roller printing the ever-growing number of patterns. Antimony was used for orange, manganese for bronze, chrome for yellow and green, and iron salt for black. In time, though, the colours faded or changed, but with the blacks the iron salt build-up made the fabric develop iron spotting, making it so brittle that these portions deteriorated until they just dropped out. That is what has happened to the Te Aroha coverlet. In 1856, however, an American, William Henry Perkin, discovered how to make synthetic dyes by using coal-tar which opened up a whole new field of more reliable dye colours for the textile market.

Following the Depression of the 1930s and the horrors of World War II, when women's minds were on matters other than patchwork, the biggest explosion of interest in patchwork and quilting ever seen burst onto the needlework scene in the mid-1970s, and spread to what appears to be every corner of the world. Happily, in the United States, and to a lesser degree the United Kingdom and New Zealand, there were still many women about who could pass on the skills of this great tradition. In the mid-1970s Ruby Short McKim's book *101 Patchwork Patterns* was the first pattern book to become available to New Zealanders who were beginning to take up patchworking and quilting as a hobby. It didn't take us long to realise that many of these patterns didn't work when using the accustomed English paper-piecing techniques, so most needlewomen quickly switched to piecing the American way. Many women

were home dressmakers, or their mothers were, so initially dress fabrics were used. But there was nowhere to buy batting or quilting thread, so some women in the latter case resorted to unravelling crochet thread to get a suitably strong thread to quilt with. By directly lobbying thread supplier Coats Paton New Zealand Ltd, we managed to get quilting thread added to the range of goods they supplied to embroidery shops.

As there were no quilting hoops, we had to improvise quilting frames; nor were there any ready-cut templates or any of the paraphernalia that the modern quilter considers to be absolutely essential equipment to even get started.

Batting too was a problem for quite a while, with some of us organising friends or relatives in America to send it to us until New Zealand manufacturers could fulfil our needs. Some of us had managed to acquire quilting hoops from abroad but only when their wives became hooked on quilting did several skilled New Zealand wood-workers eventually begin to produce quilting hoops and large floor frames. So by the time a group of Auckland quilters organised the first national patchwork and quilting symposium in 1984 we had managed to obtain samples of all manner of gadgets to enable our own versions to be made locally. Several enterprising women, however, had earlier started to supply patchwork fabrics and equipment by mail order or had opened patchwork shops.

The Quilting 'Renaissance'

The American bicentenary celebrations in the mid-1970s added great impetus to the quilting renaissance, but nobody could have predicted the tremendous chain reaction it would create throughout the world. Canada and New Zealand caught on very quickly, followed soon after by Australia. A lot of us began with the traditional patterns and English paper-piecing but quickly switched to the American piecing techniques and patterns. As we became more confident, we very soon began to expand our horizons, incorporating in our designs the colours of our surroundings, and pictures of the flora and fauna of our respective countries to give our quilts their own distinctive look. British women, by then recovered from the wartime stresses and economies and with a bit more leisure time to spare, also picked up in greater and greater numbers their old crafts, and they too began to modernise them.

The art — for it is now officially recognised in the United States as a true art form — spread to Japan, South Africa, and back to Europe. In fact there seems to be no country that hasn't joined the great universal quilting bee. Some quilts have gone from beds onto walls both in homes and in corporate office buildings, used decoratively rather than as a means of stopping draughts. In the United States antique quilts are fetching phenomenal prices at auction sales; quilt collectors are haunting home clearance sales, small antique shops, and car boot and garage sales; and museums have at last realised what treasures they have had in their storage areas. In some American towns museums devoted solely to quilts have been established, and attract continuing trails of quilters from many countries.

Such has been the burgeoning worldwide interest in the art form that many industries have built up around the craft with shops devoted only to patchwork fabrics, tools, kitsets, patterns, masses of books and magazines to serve the needs of not only long-time quilters but also many beginners. Fabric manufacturers have been very quick off the mark to produce line after line of tantalising designs, and to replicate the designs used in the prints of antique quilts and also the 1930s feed-sack patterns. These latter printed cottons were used to bag up dry goods during the Depression years in America so that once the sacks were empty the housewife had a supply of attractive cotton yardage to use for making her children's clothing or her quilts. In New Zealand, when we couldn't find just the right coloured fabric we needed, women skilled in dye techniques were soon creating fantastic colour combinations and sometimes embellishing their wares with interesting screen-printed motifs. Some women tea-dye their fabrics to give them an antique appearance while others print photographs onto their cloth for a really personal touch.

A whole array of magazines entirely devoted to quilters came onto the market with nearly every country producing their own publications. Sewing machine manufacturers have also become big winners and are making machines specially catering to quilters with all kinds of fittings to create special embellishments as well as stitches to mechanically emulate hand quilting. Quilting machines are now providing some people with the means of augmenting their income by quilting for others far more quickly than their foremothers who laboured for many long hours.

Thousands and thousands of clubs and guilds have sprung up all over the world and exhibitions abound, locally, nationally and internationally, sometimes linked to a symposium where tutors from many countries mingle to pass on their particular skill. In some countries if you haven't got access to a quilt shop from which to take lessons you may just be able to tune in to your television to find patchwork and quilting lessons. Perhaps you could afford to take one of the holiday cruises where part of the shipboard entertainment includes patchwork and quilting

classes, or if you are already a quilter you might prefer to join a tour to visit with quilters in other countries. Whatever your fancy, if it has to do with patchwork and quilting there is someone out there ready to cater to your needs. Over time, and as women eventually had better access to education, patterns and designs used in quiltmaking gradually changed. Appliqués became more sophisticated, although in more recent times some patchworkers who know how to sew fine appliqués are reverting to show that they can also make interesting primitive appliqués. With education in mathematics, the geometrics became more precise, later, manipulation of fabrics provided optical illusions so that, for instance, what appears to be a curved line is in fact a straight seam, or the placement of tones of a colour gives the impression that the viewer is looking through a transparent fabric to a darker one below. In more recent times, variations in textures give subtle changes, or pleating the fabric presents another dimension.

With the arrival of computers there are growing numbers of Internet quilters' clubs which allow women in many countries to quickly exchange ideas and new techniques. And software has become available providing quilters with the means to develop their patterns and explore colour variations before making the final decision to purchase their fabrics. Thus, while geometric patterns are universal, having their origins in people decorating or identifying their possessions or themselves, and then having been developed by those with higher learning, today's technology will bring about further advances in design. It is going to be exciting to observe what the manipulator of the machine does with those designs.

Interest in patchwork and quilting shows no signs of waning in the early years of the twenty-first century. With the rapid advancement of the technological revolution it is going to be exciting to watch what modern-day quilters are going to adapt and incorporate in their own craft. With all this speedy electronic communication, however, will the modern quilter in this self-imposed isolation have time to enjoy the same face-to-face companionship, the sharing and sometimes solving of problems, and the relaxed gentle therapy which for so long sustained many of their quilting foremothers? However, though wars are coming and going with the usual destruction they inevitably bring, and huge natural disasters continue to beset many vulnerable parts of the globe,

the smallest notice on the Internet or in a magazine stirs quilters worldwide to speedily make and assemble stacks of quilts for sending to those in need, via every imaginable form of charitable organisation. Rapid electronic communication, therefore, has already proved that even the most traditional of quilters is not averse to change.

Across all walks of life, from high-born queen to lowly peasant to practical pioneer housewife, the quilting thread has linked women's lives from generation to generation, century to century. And from proving its value on battlefields down the ages, quilting has now become a gentle art form uniting women in loving friendship, from country to country. As the old patchworkers' adage goes, 'Blessed are the quilters for they shall be known as the piecemakers.' What a formidable legacy those wonderful women around the world have left us, and what a debt we owe them for handing on to us such a loving, practical and sharing warm heritage.

Log Cabins

There does not appear to have been a custom of naming old English and European patchwork and quilting patterns or designs, apart from the obvious descriptions such as appliqués, squares, triangles, etc., for patchwork, and cross-hatching, feathers, fans, shells, etc., for quilting. When the quilts crossed the Atlantic, however, the new settler quilters began to give their traditional designs names, possibly the better to let their friends and relations at a distance know precisely what pattern they were using for their latest quilt. Many new patterns came into being as, with their expanding horizons, they saw all manner of wonderful flowers, unfamiliar animals and birds and perhaps Indian designs to inspire them, and somewhere along the way they decided to give them names. As the patterns were passed around, over time some of the new designs, and old ones as well, accumulated a variety of names. In some cases the same pattern could have up to half a dozen different titles, and variations of the patterns or their setting together would have an extra few words added, such as Barn Raising Log Cabin, Straight Furrows Log Cabin or Sunshine and Shadows Log Cabin.

The Log Cabin is an example of a traditional English pattern that had been used long before it crossed the Atlantic but only acquired its name in North America. The basic pieced block pattern, which consisted of a square scrap of fabric surrounded by strips, looked so much like the settlers' first dwellings, enclosing a square with rows of logs butting each other at the corners, that the name Log Cabin seemed a grand way to describe it.

Apart from the old hexagon quilts by far the most frequent pattern located in New Zealand is the Log Cabin. Many of these have been made using shirting cottons, which leads one to think the quilters may have had access to off-cut scraps from factories where some of them may even have been employed.

There are many examples of the Log Cabin pattern amongst the old quilts found in New Zealand. There tends to be little difference between many of these, which have used the customary layout of the finished blocks (side by side in rows) and have frequently been made of shirting materials. However, there are also some fine examples of several of the more spectacular settings of this popular pattern.

A Log Cabin design on point, that could be described as a 'light and shadow' checkerboard design, from the collection of Broadgreen House, Nelson.

Anna Hunger's Quilt

This is a rather primitive old Log Cabin quilt thought to have been made around 1830. It was purchased by the current owner at an estate sale in 1987 and is believed to have been made by Mrs Anna Hunger. The Hunger family, who were early farming settlers in the Normanby district of Taranaki, came from Switzerland. As the quilt has been altered over the years, it is not known whether Anna originally made it before she came to New Zealand, but some of the fabrics used in the top have been dated as being from around 1830. That suggests that she either made it before emigrating from Switzerland or brought a whole lot of scraps with her, for she certainly would not have been able to purchase them in New Zealand at that time. However, the backing, at least, was hand sewn in this country; it was constructed from flour and oatmeal bags which depict the trademark names of goods produced in New Zealand, as well as cut-down old pyjamas and tablecloths.

A wide variety of cottons — red, white, several shades of blue, yellow, green, black, brown, grey, tan, maroon, pink and lavender — were used to make the log cabin blocks, which vary in size between 7″ and 8″. The construction also varies: in every alternate row the blocks are placed on point, and this has necessitated the use of corner triangles to square them off. There are 60 blocks, featuring a mixture of solids, stripes, prints, plaids, polka dots and florals, in the same colours as the cottons which have been used. Though the squares and strips are uneven, the placement of the colours is quite pleasing. The ten rows of six blocks give an overall size of roughly 47″ by 77″, but the original quilt was much bigger. As is often the case with Log Cabins, there is no batting, but the two layers are quilted together using back stitching, although this may be construction stitches when sewing the strips onto the base fabric squares. When discovered, at the time of the sale, the quilt was being used as an under-blanket between the wire-wove and mattress of a single bed, and still had the tying-down strings attached. It had probably been used as an under-blanket for many years; consequently, there is some rusting to the lining fabrics.

Detail of the primitive piecing and fabrics of Anna Hunger's Log Cabin quilt.

A Log Cabin quilt partly made by Anna Hunger circa 1830 prior to emigrating from Switzerland to New Zealand. The lining is made from New Zealand flour and oatmeal bags. 47" x 77"

Onehunga Fencible Cottage Quilt

In 1847–48, when there was much unrest in the Colony, the government of the day established four military frontier settlements at Howick, Panmure, Otahuhu and Onehunga to protect the growing town of Auckland. The British Army ex-Regulars who were recruited (many of whom had served in India and some possibly at Crimea) had to be available at a moment's notice to take up arms in defence of the town. In return, they were granted land and either a cottage or half a cottage, both the land allotment and the size of the dwelling depending on their rank. These military men were later to be known as the Fencibles and their dwellings as Fencible cottages. One of the Onehunga Fencible cottages, which is now a small colonial museum, has amongst its small collection of quilts a very fine Log Cabin quilt (circa 1860) that is believed to have been one of the possessions of a Fencible family coming from India. Judging from the quality of the fabrics and the needlework used, the head of the house was likely to have been an officer rather than a private.

The quilt measures 69″ by 70″ including the 6½″ border of very worn red velvet, which has an elegantly designed handmade lace and tape overlay made from coarse white cotton and gold thread. The blocks of the log cabin are set so that where the pale colours of four blocks come together pointed crosses are formed, and the four sets of dark colours form squares. Although the individual blocks are set in straight lines, the dark sets give the appearance of the squares being on point. The 5½″ blocks all have a central square of red velvet upon which at some later stage someone has embroidered in yellow wool a simple straight-stitch daisy. This 'embellishment' seems out of place when viewing the fabrics used in constructing the blocks. The light strips are pale gold, cream and white, and the darker ones are red, black, dark green, medium and dark blues, the fabrics used being grosgrain, satin, velvet and brocades. The dark grosgrain may have come from the trims on an army officer's jacket. The quilt is obviously the work of a skilled needlewoman.

Detail of Onehunga Fencible Cottage Log Cabin quilt, showing added woollen daisies.

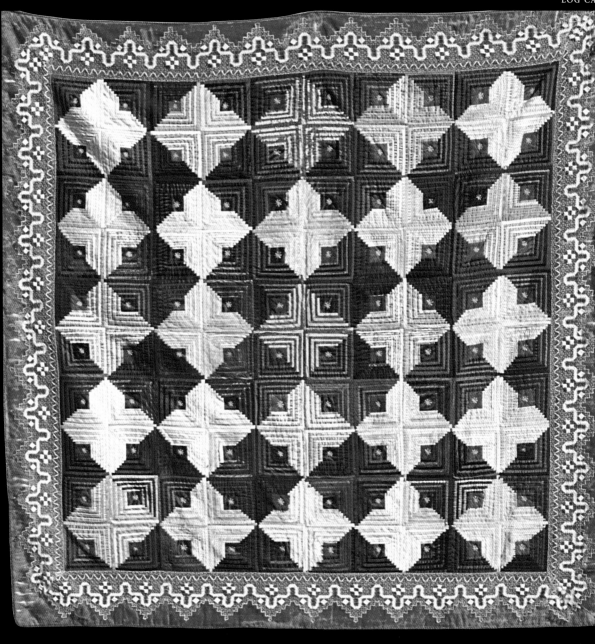

Onehunga Fencible Cottage Log Cabin quilt with detail of the lace overlay on the red velvet border.
69″ x 70″

The Auckland War Memorial Museum Quilt

The Auckland War Memorial Museum also has in its collection a Log Cabin quilt from the Victorian era. There is no provenance for this quilt but there is a similarity in the construction of blocks with the Onehunga Fencible cottage quilt, although the standard of workmanship is not as high. However, the placement of the blocks in the Barn Raising set (the dark colours form frames which resemble the wooden construction frames when building a barn) makes this a dramatic quilt, and the way the dark frames are so forceful and somewhat overwhelmingly sombre raises the possibility that this may have been intended as a mourning quilt, although there is no date or inscription to verify this.

Auckland War Memorial Museum's Victorian Log Cabin quilt pieced together in a Barn Raising set and lined with red satin. 46" x 46"

Detail of the above quilt illustrating the variety of fabrics used.

Whakatane District Museum and Gallery Quilt

This version of a Log Cabin coverlet was presented to the Whakatane Museum by members of the family of a gentleman who had been a District Commissioner in the Pacific Islands. It has been sewn by machine from the typical plain cotton fabric used in the making of tivaevae quilts. The piecing of the central squares using the Windmill pattern is very inaccurate but they, together with the setting of the completed blocks, give this coverlet the appearance of a lot of movement. The bright colours used and the general effect of movement lend this bedcover an exuberantly happy feeling.

Whakatane District Museum and Gallery's Log Cabin coverlet was made in the Pacific Islands. No date is available but the cotton colours are typical of 1930s fabrics.

Detail of the Pacific Islands Log Cabin quilt.

Hexagons, Diamonds & Other English Piecing

The many ways quilters had used hexagons and diamonds were hitherto referred to as mosaic because all the one-shape-and-size pieces resembled the old mosaic floors and religious pictures favoured by many ancient civilisations, including the Romans. However, once the colours of the fabric scraps used began, by the manipulation of skilled fingers, to reveal what looked like a flower, or a three-dimensional square block, along came the names Flower Garden, Grandmother's Flower Garden, Honeycomb, Baby's Blocks or Tumbling Blocks, Field of Diamonds, and so on.

Because the one-patch patterns used hexagons, diamonds and octagons (the last also requiring a square to join them together), the pieces had to be very precisely measured or they would not fit together properly. Thus the technique of making a meticulously measured and cut template came into being, from which paper shapes were cut. The fabrics were then cut ¼″ larger on all sides and used to cover the paper template by turning the seam allowance to the back of the paper and tacking it in place, and then the units were whip stitched together, hence giving rise to the name paper piecing. To some this technique is also known as English piecing as it was greatly favoured by the British needlewomen. Many of the old surviving patchwork coverlets and quilts in New Zealand have been made by this method. Their designs are usually hexagons or diamonds, although quilts using other shapes have been found where, because of the precision necessary, papers have obviously been used. Some tops have not been lined and have the papers still in place, which has been a great boon in dating the work as frequently dates appear on letters, documents or publications from which the lining papers have been cut. Some of the coverlets that have been lined also still have papers left in. The reasoning behind this is a moot point. Was it for extra warmth when wool or cotton batting was not available? Was it to give the top a bit of body and make it smoother, and to prevent the shapes, which of necessity had some sides cut on the bias, from stretching? Or did the maker simply not think it was important to remove the papers? It was important, because when the coverlet needed to be laundered the papers started to disintegrate. One quilt featured — made by Elisa McPherson (see page 66) — that must have had the papers left in, around the edges if not the whole top, for that area of the quilt feels as though it has chewed-up papier mâché inside it.

Paper piecing was very popular for the patchworker who was going on a long journey, whether by coach or covered wagon, or by sailing ship to a far distant land. The templates and fabrics could be pre-cut, put into workbaskets, small boxes or fabric bags and kept close to hand for the women to pick up and put down as and when the long hours of travel became too boring. Most of these women would also be accustomed to not sit idling away the minutes and hours; they would normally keep some form of sewing, knitting, crochet or tatting nearby to pick up

at a moment's notice. At least one of the quilts, that documented and shown on page 74, was made on the voyage from England to New Zealand, and others were started and worked upon during the voyage, but possibly not completed until after arrival.

Elizabeth Fry, the English Quaker preacher, philanthropist and prison reformer who worked so hard to improve conditions for women prisoners in Newgate and other prisons throughout England, and who founded hostels for the homeless, was known to have organised patchwork sewing kits for women convicts headed for Tasmania and other Australian convict settlements. Probably simple squares of fabric, more easily stitched by women who possibly had few or no needle skills, these kits would afford them something to occupy the long days and ease the appalling transportation conditions. With a bit of

Detail from Maria Hackworth's quilt (page 74) showing a typical array of prints used in hexagon 'all over' designs.

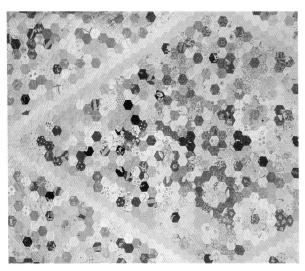

Traditional Flower Garden pattern with Turkey red used to advantage amongst the multi-coloured cotton hexagons.

luck and diligence, a kit would also provide a woman who persevered with her sewing with a colourful bedcover to brighten the hard life she could expect upon arrival.

Up until the time when the paper piecing method came into vogue, patchwork in the British Isles had been to a large extent made with various geometric shapes frequently set to form borders around a central medallion, or appliqués which could also be in medallion form. There are some excellent examples of medallion quilts in New Zealand.

Another type of quilt which tested the needlewoman's skills was the whole-cloth quilt, frequently referred to as a Durham quilt, although the quilters of Wales, Cumbria and other parts of Britain were also very highly skilled in this form of quilting. The whole-cloth quilt consists of one large sheet of plain fabric (although this may have needed to have been pieced together to get the required size) batted with wool, lined, and then closely quilted all over using an amazing array of designs, usually in the same colour thread, though sometimes a contrasting colour would be used. Wool was mostly used for batting in the British quilts as, especially in the country areas, this was the most readily obtainable ingredient for the filling in the quilt sandwich. Often, though not always, the quilters, especially of the whole-cloth quilts, worked in groups around a large frame — the forerunner of the famous American quilting bees.

More often than not this was also a source of income.

Some men were involved in the business of quiltmaking, too, as itinerant quilt markers. These men had many and varied intricate quilting-design templates, were very skilled at marking the patterns on these large whole-cloth quilts, and travelled from village to village earning their living at undertaking this rather onerous task. They thus allowed the quilters more time to concentrate on their sewing.

Of two quilts documented in Hawke's Bay, one was from Durham and one from Cumbria. They had been made by the owner's grandmother and mother and given to her when, as a World War II war bride, she sailed to New Zealand to join her husband. Her family could trace its lineage right back to 1066 when her ancestors arrived in England as part of William the Conqueror's retinue. For services to the king they were granted land in the county of Durham and began farming. The house they built is a fortified slate-roofed stone building of two storeys with walls a metre thick. Situated at Garrigill near Alston, the farm is called Lonning Head, because a lonning is a public walkway across the countryside and the house was at the head or end of the path. The owner of the quilts has a pen-and-ink postcard-type picture of the old farmhouse with a cross marking the room in which her grandmother did her quilting.

The two quilts had the most awe-inspiring quilting. One had been yellow and the other blue,

An example of the Diamond Stars pattern. The quilt is owned by Mrs Colleen Hareb, who found it in a New Plymouth op shop. The maker is unknown. 46" x 96"

This dainty pillowslip, which is one of a pair at the Onehunga Fencible Cottage, uses Turkey red in a pleasing way to provide a bright backing for the yoyos, though they would probably have been known to the maker as Suffolk puffs.

and the batting was of wool. However, from much use and many, many washings they became very worn and faded, with just hints of their original colours showing up in the valleys of the quilting, while the raised surfaces had worn so much the wool was showing through in many parts. Unfortunately photographs do not reveal the beauty of these two quilts, which had been made with such love and used to the full for their intended purpose.

Suffolk puffs, in America known as Yoyos, represent another form of needlework broadly coming under the heading of patchwork. This is a method of cutting circles of fabric, running a gathering thread around the circumference and pulling the circle into a pleated or gathered circle. These are joined together at several points and then mounted onto a large piece of coloured backing fabric. The pillow sham above is a good example of

how effective this technique can look. It comprises white cotton puffs mounted on a Turkey red backing (see page 124 for the history of Turkey red cotton).

A photograph was submitted to the writer of what looks like a quite spectacular Suffolk puff quilt, but unfortunately the person who sent the photograph and story had lost the name and address of the owner so it is not possible to publish the photograph here without permission.

The quilt had been made by an earlier generation of the owner's family and was known as The Naughty Quilt because the children of the family, whenever they had been naughty, had to make a required number of gathered circles as punishment. From the apparent size of the quilt they must have been very, very naughty children indeed, or maybe there were lots of siblings.

Ann Eliza Ellis (née Izod, 1839–91)

Ann Eliza Izod was born in Bracknell, Berkshire, England in 1839, and in the year 1864, shortly after her marriage to George Coxon Ellis, who was by profession a chemist, the young bride left England, family and friends, to follow her husband for better or worse, for richer or poorer. Little could this young gentlewoman have visualised the extraordinarily adventurous life ahead of her, nor the many lonely hours and sometimes frightening experiences with which she would have to cope. They sailed from Plymouth on the *Golden Hind* bound for Australia, landing at Brisbane, Queensland, on 5 January 1865 and then settling in the little country township of Roma where George practised his profession for two years before deciding to come to New Zealand. Here they farmed land at Taotaoroa in the isolated backblocks of Cambridge, Waikato, but this venture was not very successful. George had been in correspondence with a relative by marriage of his wife, John T. Arundell, a South Pacific trader and copra dealer whose London-based company also prospected and worked the rich phosphate guano deposits on several of the islands around the Gulf of Carpentaria and the Great Barrier Reef.

Leaving his wife to supervise the formal education of their four sons, James, George, Albert and Ernest, and cope with the management of the farm and hired help, George would disappear for months on end to travel around the various copra plantations and guano

Ann Eliza Ellis

works of John T. Arundell to familiarise himself with the workings of the company. On returning to New Zealand he would arrive with sacks of phosphate, which would be barged up the Waikato River to Cambridge and then to the farm. Once the fertiliser was spread around the hills and fields of the farm, the land began to flourish, but by this time George had officially joined the company and was managing the copra plantations on several islands. James, the oldest son, later joined the company and within a few years George and Bert were also recruited. Ernest, unfortunately, died in his late teens when he contracted tuberculosis.

When she left England, in her luggage Ann Eliza had packed snippets of materials (mainly silks) given

The memory quilt made by Ann Ellis
circa 1869–70 while living at Taotaoroa
farm near Cambridge. 76″ by 66″

to her by family and friends and during the long, lonely evenings on the farm she began to sort these bright fabric mementos into little piles and then enclose the cut pieces safely in little cotton bags. Memories must have flooded back when she recognised a piece of fabric and recalled the friend or relative who had given it to her and the occasion upon which such and such a dress had been worn. Pangs of homesickness must have been added to her sense of loneliness and feelings of isolation. After months and years of being hidden away, the silks, velvets, cottons and ribbons in a multitude of designs were revealed with none of their brightness diminished and inspired Ann to begin to make her wonderful memory quilt. She chose a traditional English design of six pointed stars and the hundreds of stars in her galaxy were linked together with black velvet diamonds to form hexagons. The starry area measures 53″ x 44″ and is edged with a 1 1/2″ narrow black velvet frame, which is then surrounded by four rows of 2″ squares and half-square triangles on point, each seam being covered by a 1/4″ strip of black velvet. This border is followed by a row of 3″ squares on point and finally a dashing garnet-coloured silken fringe 4″ deep. The quilt, which measures 76″ by 66″, has no batting and is lined with a lovely deep rose glazed cotton.

Because of her way of life, Ann possibly never used this lovely bedcover after she had made it, which is probably why after all these years its colours are still bright. The fabrics, though, have become rather fragile, partly due to the fact that, as with many of the English pieced quilts in New Zealand, the paper templates have been left attached to the fabrics and the sharp edges are beginning to cut the woven threads. This is a wonderful memento of a very brave, devoted, loving wife and mother; a gentle woman, who deserves to be remembered for how she coped with a life which was not easy, frequently put her and her family in danger but did not break her indomitable spirit.

By the time the farm was sold, Ann's husband was managing several plantations on various islands and her sons were working on other islands with several young Niuean men as assistants. Supplies, mainly of ship's biscuits and rice, would be dropped off by schooner at regular or sometimes irregular intervals, depending on the vagaries of the weather. The family would augment their diet with fish and whatever fruit and vegetables would be growing locally. Ann Eliza travelled with her men and her way of life changed greatly as she sailed by schooner from one group of islands to another, living in the established camps which sometimes had the luxury of a hut or cottage. She would be forever packing and unpacking and after her daily chores were done would occupy her time combing the beach for pretty pieces of coral, colourful shells and brightly hued crab-backs, or sit for a while to study the fascinating bird-life.

In 1888, when Ann was visiting her son Bert on Baker Island where he was employed in the Company's laboratory, a hurricane-force storm blew up and the mountainous seas swept away the wharf and houses, leaving a scene of chaos and destruction. However, these intrepid, adventurous people appeared to be able to cope with any setback. Some time later, when life had apparently returned to some normality, the schooner *Olive* arrived with her husband, and she and George had a couple of peaceful months together before they unexpectedly received another visit from the *Olive* bearing news of a terrible accident to their son George. James, George junior and a party of Niuean boys were engaged in planting at Howland Island and as the boys were not catching enough fish George went with them to the reef with a charge of dynamite to speed things up, but the charge was faulty. No mention is made of injuries suffered by the Niuean boys but George was grievously injured.

There was no means of communication in this isolated place and certainly no medical care, so James did his best and poured oil onto the wounds. George had lost an arm and an eye; his jaw had been half blown away; his nose was damaged; and he had sustained deep wounds to his neck and chest, resulting subsequently in the loss of the use of one lung. For ten days James cared for his severely injured brother until the *Olive* arrived and took the two

young men to Baker Island where Ann was hurriedly embarked and the ship sailed on for Apia, normally five sailing days away. However they were becalmed, and then endured a bad storm, so an extra ten days were added to their journey. Ann did not leave her son's side, nursing, comforting and caring for the seriously injured young man in the confines of a small cabin. Two crewmen helped with the lifting of the

Detail showing some of the fabrics on Ann Ellis's quilt.

patient and James continued to assist with the regular changing of dressings. Though George was kept as mobile as possible his lung was in a critical state by the time they eventually arrived at Apia. After five weeks of medical care there, Ann and her son were able to set sail for Sydney. As if the stress and worry over her son were not enough to break her spirit, while she was in Apia Ann had received a letter bearing the sad news of her father's death. She must have found it difficult to hand her son over to others after the many weeks of constant nursing care she had given him, and great praise and admiration were heaped on her by the amazed Sydney doctors who took over the vital hospital care that was needed to restore George's shattered body. After many more weeks of hospitalisation Ann and George were able to travel to Auckland, where Ernest was awaiting their arrival.

The trio spent nearly two enjoyable months with relatives and friends before joining the schooner *Ryko* for the return voyage to Howland Island. This time they were able to take with them their possessions that had been in storage for many years.

Although this ship provided Ann with a cleaned cabin, apart from some unwashed crockery, there was an ominous nasty smell that proved to come from a severe infestation of cockroaches. These would not have been the ordinary cockroaches occasionally found in houses here but the larger tropical variety,

so it isn't any wonder Ann didn't think it funny to awake one night to find six of these creatures on her pillow.

After just over three weeks of pleasant sailing a sudden squall hit the schooner, snapping its foremast in two places and sweeping away part of the mast. Several squalls continued to hit the rolling vessel while all hands were frantically working on the damaged mast and torn sails. A week later in calm weather they were able to raise the makeshift mast and repaired sails and were once more on course, though at a slower speed.

When they finally arrived at Howland Island, Ann Eliza was delighted to find not the one-room abode she had become accustomed to but a little house of two rooms, with a small room for bathing and the luxury of verandas at the front and back. What a wonderful welcome home her family had provided for her after an absence of nearly a year devoted to unstinting loving care, patience and understanding, dedicated to restoring the mental and physical well-being of her son. What pleasure she must have found in unpacking the many boxes of long-hidden treasures and arranging them about her new home.

Ann had at least one trip back to England, and the occasional break in Auckland and Cambridge, as well as her shorter trips to the various islands where her sons were working. On returning home after one of her holidays she was not very happy to find that the constant war against rats had not been maintained during her absence and there had been a population explosion of the vermin. Sixty were caught in the house, eight of them in her bedroom.

Around this time it was decided that, as the guano deposits they had been working were virtually exhausted, the company would form a new base and concentrate on working the deposits on Raine Island, over 3,000 kilometres away in the Barrier Reef off the Queensland coast. This was a major undertaking as all the houses and buildings had to be dismantled and loaded onto a ship together with all the laboratory and carpentry equipment. The decks were piled high with cases of equipment and furnishings, timber, a large ship's buoy, boats, punts and tanks. It took seventeen days to make the journey and the first sight of their destination was the Raine Island beacon, looking for all the world like a giant castle from a chess set. Landing was delayed for several days due to adverse currents and weather conditions. A camp was set up on shore and within a few days other ships arrived from Australia with Chinese and Malay labourers, timber and supplies. The mammoth task of setting up this new base was hampered to a certain extent when the wells which were dug produced only brackish, undrinkable water, necessitating the construction of a makeshift condensation plant which served its purpose for seven months until a proper condenser was brought in by ship.

Ann's life at this new base was a decided improvement. She had a proper house built from new timber, and as they were not too distant from the mainland and ships called fairly regularly, supplies were more readily obtainable, enabling her to make pretty curtains to complement the pictures she was able to hang on the walls and the shelves provided to display her porcelain ornaments. She was a great homemaker and accustomed to making shirts and trousers for her menfolk; she recorded in her writings the making of pillowcases, and table napkins for the mess room. There were new species of birds to watch and the familiar turtles. During her rambles around the beaches, accompanied by her little dog, she could study the marine life and coral formations — different from those she was accustomed to seeing elsewhere in the Pacific waters — and add to her wonderful and diverse shell collection. The company finished its work on Raine Island in 1892, whereupon all the houses and equipment had to be removed.

However, in June of 1891, after a brief illness Ann Eliza Ellis died at age 52 and was laid to rest in a lonely grave under the shadow of the huge stone beacon. Isolated, windswept Raine Island subsequently came under the care of the Queensland government and as part of a marine reserve is maintained by a corporation which also keeps Ann's grave, and that of one other person interred nearby, in a neat and tidy order.

Elisa McPherson (née Squire, 1842–1933)

Elisa McPherson, wearing a large hat, second from left, standing next to her husband far left.

In 1842 chemist and teacher William Squire and his wife sailed from London aboard an English ship carrying pioneers bound for New Zealand. During the voyage their daughter Elisa was born. The family settled at Wakefield, Nelson and Elisa lived her entire 91 years in that district. She married John Gordon McPherson, a builder and wheelwright, and bore him five sons and four daughters. Elisa must have been an excellent housewife and mother to manage such a large family and yet find time to make many quilts. Her grandson Colonel H.J.G. Low of Taupo, who owns the quilt pictured opposite, recalls that every bed had quilts, and besides the one he inherited there are still several more being cherished by other family members. Elisa was a smart dresser and judging from photographs of family weddings had a great love of large stylish hats.

Colonel Low's quilt is believed to have been made between 1872 and 1882 and was hand sewn in the traditional manner with paper templates using diamond shapes, which were almost as popular as the hexagons favoured by so many of the Victorian patchworkers. The quilt measures 45″ x 58″ and the diamonds, 2″ wide by 4″ long, are arranged pleasantly in an all-over pattern. The fabrics are a mixture of cottons, wool, crepe, linen and flannel and feature a wide variety of colours in solids, stripes, prints, plaids, checks, polka dots and chintz. The lining is made up of flour bags hand-stitched together. There is no batting or quilting, and the papers appear to have been left in place around the edges at least, though the rest may have disintegrated from frequent laundering. Those at the edges have really wadded together and feel almost as solid as papier mâché. There are a few rust marks on the backing. These could have come from the wire of the clothes-line or the quilt may, at some time, have been used as an under-blanket between the mattress and the wire-wove of a bed base.

English paper pieced diamond pattern quilt using a wide variety of fabrics, lined with flour bags but with no batting or quilting. Made between 1872–82 by Elisa McPherson at Nelson. 45" x 58"

The Holt Coverlet (circa 1853)

Elizabeth Bancroft was born on 9 May 1835, probably at home in Sawpit Street, Dunham Massey, Cheshire, England, and James Holt is believed to have been born on 29 September 1834 in the same district. As they were both Primitive Methodists their families were probably well acquainted with each other through church.

Elizabeth became betrothed to James in 1853. He was a brickmaker by trade and as there is no indication that she was employed in any trade it can be assumed that she occupied her time in assisting her mother in the general running of the family home. According to family history the young couple spent many hours in the two years before their wedding creating together a wonderful patchwork coverlet for their matrimonial bed. It is one of the rare instances recorded of a man being involved in the actual sewing of a quilt.

Measuring 87″ by 98″, it is made of cotton in a medallion form, and although it is almost primitive in the irregularity of some of the shapes used, other areas are quite exact in their cutting and sewing. The central oblong has pieced hexagon flowers in each corner, a variety of other geometric shapes scattered about and, besides some appliqué chintz pieces depicting cherubs, the couple have also appliquéd in pink 'J & E HOLT'. This oblong is framed with a border of Turkey red and mixed cotton prints in a sawtooth pattern. The remainder of the top is made up of bands of squares and oblongs in a wide variety of prints interspersed with two more sawtooth frames. There is no lining to this charming coverlet. James and Elizabeth Holt were married on 15 October 1855 at Rostherne Church and in later life also celebrated their golden wedding at the same church. They produced seven children — Samuel Bancroft, Alex, Albert, Harry, Fred, Annie and Edith. The coverlet was inherited by Samuel who, following the death of his parents, came to New Zealand aboard the steamship *Rotorua* in 1923, bringing the bedcover with him. In 1927 Samuel and Emma Holt settled in Otorohanga, and in 1944 the coverlet was passed on to their great-niece Mrs Nellie Glossop. During a bad flood which struck Otorohanga in 1958, Nellie's home was for some time inundated by silt-laden flood waters to a depth of two metres. What treatment the poor coverlet had Nellie did not know, although today the top shows no water stains and the fragility of some of the fabrics is mainly from age. Overcome by all she had to manage in the cleaning up of her home she handed the bedcover over to her aunt and uncle, the son of Samuel and Emma Holt. When Mrs Emma Holt gave up her home to go into a pensioner flat, Nellie suggested to the family that perhaps they would be willing to donate the coverlet to the Otorohanga Museum which was then in the process of being formed, and this suggestion was agreed to. Subsequent to documenting this quilt, a fire at the museum meant that the quilt suffered some smoke damage. It is now in the care of Nellie Glossop's neice in Kerikeri.

An unlined cotton medallion coverlet made by J. and E. Holt in 1853–54 prior to their marriage in 1855. 87" x 98"

Elizabeth Myra Renall (née Luxton, 1881–1961)

Elizabeth Myra Renall in her honeymoon attire.

Myra's father, William Thomas Luxton, a farm labourer, was born on 2 March 1849 at Chawleigh, England and left London on 27 July 1875 on board the *Himalaya* bound for Lyttelton, New Zealand, where he arrived on 17 November of that year. On 6 May 1878 he married Elizabeth Ellen Frost, who had been born at Rangiora on 13 April 1855, her parents Joseph and Elizabeth having arrived in New Zealand some years earlier on the *Grasmere*.

After their marriage William and Ellen settled in Wellington, where William took up work with a meat company and later acquired his own butchery business. Myra was the eldest of six children born to William and Ellen, the other children being William Thomas, Joseph Henry, Edward George (who died when he was seventeen months old), Myrtle Elsie and Stanley George. The children were all born and educated in Wellington. When in 1900 the marriage broke down and Myra's parents parted, her father returned to Christchurch where he lived until his death in 1914.

The practical Ellen and her family shifted to Makara, where a dairy farm was bought and run with the help of the children. They would rise early in the morning to hand milk the cows, and then the milk would be delivered by horse and cart to the doors of Wellington residents. Myra, now a young woman, had completed her education to standard seven level and had trained as a teacher under the guidance of the

head teachers, which was the custom of the time. During her training she would ride on horseback each day from Makara to Karori, a journey of 10 kilometres each way. As she was a talented piano player Myra was often called upon by the local residents to provide the music for a night of dancing at the Makara Hall.

In 1904 Myra Luxton was appointed to the position of teacher at Ponatahi School, a few miles from Carterton in the Wairarapa. Eager to commence her duties she arrived in Carterton by the afternoon train from Wellington; expecting to be met by some bewhiskered member of the school committee, she failed to recognise as her escort a shy young schoolboy who had been despatched to the station to conduct her to her new abode. The envoy returned home minus Miss Luxton, telling his parents that he could not recognise any disembarking passenger resembling a 'school-marm' — an easy mistake to make, for the new school-marm was a petite, pretty young woman not at all resembling what the young man expected.

Undaunted, after having made enquiries about her destination, Myra hired a horse and trap from Cole's Stables, and, driven by another schoolboy, set out for Ponatahi. She called in at the Renall homestead to find the family engaged in cooking the evening meal — outside, for the chimneys of the house had been demolished in a recent earthquake and had not yet been replaced. Introducing herself as the new teacher, Myra enquired where she was to board and was directed to the Tilson homestead. She eventually arrived at her destination after an arduous journey, the last two hours having been spent in darkness except for the glimmering light of candles in the gig lamps.

This was not an auspicious start to her teaching career. It was arranged later that Miss Luxton should board at the Renall homestead, much to the displeasure of Harold, one of the sons of the family, who did not relish the prospect of having a school-marm boarding with the family. However, Myra fitted in so well that she soon came to be considered one of the family — to such an extent that some eighteen months later she resigned her teaching position to become Mrs Harold Robert Richmond Renall.

At the time of the wedding, which was held at Makara, Wellington on 7 February 1906, Myra was 24 years of age and her husband 21. For their honeymoon trip the young couple travelled on the *Mararoa* to Christchurch, where doubtless they would have taken the opportunity to call upon Myra's father. Later that year Harold bought a farm at Dalefield and their first daughter, Erina Jane, was born the following year in Carterton. In 1910 Harold and his brother Herbert acquired farmland further north at Mount Bruce, near Eketahuna, and as there was no house on the property Myra and their daughter returned to Makara to stay with her mother while Harold began to build their home. In due course he sent for his wife who, upon arrival, was shocked to find that the only floorboards in the bedroom were where the bed stood. Their second daughter, Myra Nona, was born in Eketahuna in 1910.

Deciding to try something different, Harold moved Myra and his family to Taranaki, where they lived in Inglewood, then Waitara and later New Plymouth. He took up employment with the firm of Newton King, installing milking machines and water pumps. Their third daughter, Patricia Myrtle, was born in 1916 in New Plymouth. However, in 1919 when Harold's parents retired, he, Myra and their three daughters returned to Kokotau where, in 1920, their only son, Harold Luxton, was born.

Myra's life as a farmer's wife was a busy one, often providing meals for many more than her own family. Like many country wives she was not wasteful, and thrifty practices were part of the way of life. Flour bags were saved and sewn into pillowcases, and she probably also used sugar bags to make her oven cloths. She crocheted a white cotton bedspread for her own bed and also did embroidery and knitting. However for real relaxation she would always turn to music and spend some time playing her piano.

Myra made at least one quilt, a utility quilt (54″ by 53½″) for her son Luxton, and it was used for many years on his iron bed. It was customary during those years for gentlemen to have their suits made by the local tailor. The client would select the fabric from samples of suiting material provided by the tailor. It was from tailor's samples that Myra made her son's quilt.

The sturdy woollen suiting samples she chose were oblong pieces which, when sewn together, were 3¼″ x 4¼″ in size and were of solid colours, stripes or plaids in dark shades of blue, green, brown, grey and black. After the oblongs were sewn together in rows, to enhance and brighten the top Myra embroidered each seam line with feather stitch in assorted colours,

mainly cream, red and yellow. She used a folded grey blanket as batting, and for the backing chose a bright cretonne curtaining with a large print depicting bunches of flowers, leaves and birds. Though the woollen fabrics used in making the top tend to be somewhat scratchy, the cotton backing would have been much softer against the face. The quilt, which was warm and heavy, measures 54″ x 53½″.

Sadly for Myra and Harold their only son, Second Lieutenant Harold Luxton Renall, was killed in March 1944 during the battle for Monte Cassino, Italy, during World War II. Myra died in 1961 and the quilt was passed first to her daughter Myra Nona, and then on to the latter's daughter Elizabeth Nona Hayes. Today, although it has had a lot of use as a warm bed cover, and then as an under-blanket between the mattress and the wire-wove on several beds, the quilt is in quite good condition. There are a few rust marks from the wire-wove, some of the feather stitching is beginning to disintegrate, and there is a certain amount of unevenness on the edges due to laundering and some of the construction fabrics shrinking more than others. Although the quilt is not a thing of beauty, as a utility bedcover it has most certainly stood the test both of purpose and time.

The story of Elizabeth Myra (Luxton) Renall was provided by her granddaughter Elizabeth Nona Hayes who, being a quilter herself, treasures the quilt made by her grandmother as part of her family history.

Utility quilt made by Elizabeth Myra Renall, circa 1930 from woollen suiting samples. It is batted with a blanket and lined with cretonne curtaining fabric. The surface is feather stitch embroidery over construction seams. 54" x 53½"

Maria Hackworth

In September 1855 Maria Hackworth, a widow accompanied by her two young children, sailed from England aboard the *Queen of England*, bound for Australia. Amongst the passengers were a number of civil servants being transferred to Australia, but Maria's destination was New Zealand where she was to wed her late husband's brother, Captain John Hackworth of the New Zealand Constabulary. The final stage of this voyage was by the schooner *Cheetah*, which sailed regularly from Australia to Wellington.

During the long voyage from England Maria passed a lot of time sewing 1047 2″ hexagons, first to paper templates in the traditional English patchwork technique, and then into a hexagon Grandmother's Flower Garden shape surrounded by sixteen further rows of hexagons. This large hexagon-shaped medallion reached the size of 66″ from point to point and 56½″ from straight edge to straight edge. To make it usable as a bedcover it was then sewn onto an oblong of bright blue cotton.

Maria used a very wide variety of colours of cotton in prints, stripes, checks and polka dots. Some of the material has been pieced together to make it large enough to cut the shapes. The papers have been left in place, and those discernible around the edges appear to have been cut from documents such as accounts or ticket receipts for the hiring of horses; one is from some kind of form from a paymaster to do with the transfer of merchandise or land. Perhaps these were

some of the accounts and receipts Maria received when she was settling up her affairs and transferring her belongings for shipping to New Zealand. For its age (having been made in 1855) the coverlet, though worn, repaired, and fragile in some parts, has stood the test of time quite well.

In 1939 two elderly ladies, Misses Evelyn and Ethel Hackworth, who said they were direct descendants of the maker (surely the two children who sailed with Maria), brought the coverlet to the organisers of the Centennial Exhibition held in Wellington in 1939–40. As the blue surround cloth was fragile and would not hold the patchwork for display it was removed and replaced by an exact matching coloured mount of Indian cloth. After the exhibition was over the two ladies, who had no living relatives, gave the coverlet to Ruth Flashoff of Havelock North, who subsequently passed it on to its present owner, Mrs Eileen Gower, a collector of old dolls, teddy-bears, toys and memorabilia of childhood.

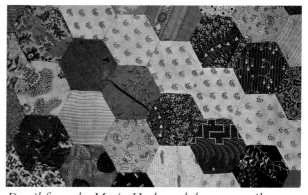

Detail from the Maria Hackworth hexagon quilt.

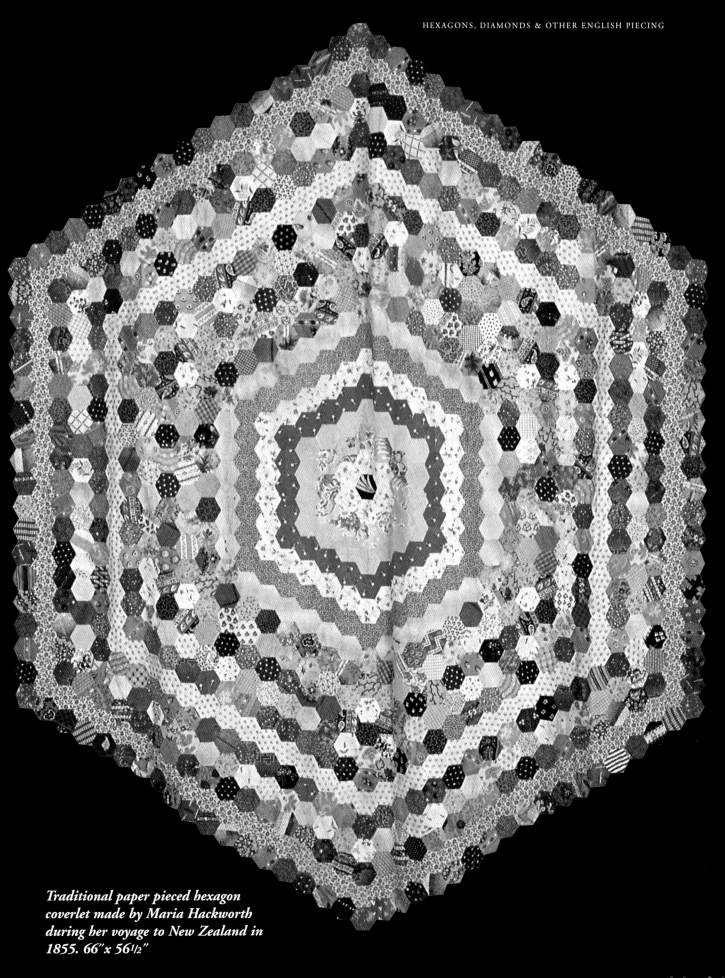

*Traditional paper pieced hexagon
coverlet made by Maria Hackworth
during her voyage to New Zealand in
1855. 66"x 56½"*

Linda Constance Monro (1894–1963)

Linda in the battery-powered wheelchair purchased in 1946.

Linda Monro was born into a family which can trace its history back to the seventeenth century and which had a long association with the medical profession. Three generations in succession held the Chair of Anatomy at the University of Edinburgh over a period of 126 years, and then the mould was broken: in 1842, Linda's grandfather, Dr David Monro, emigrated to New Zealand. He settled in Nelson and although he still occasionally practised medicine this was not to be his main source of income. Having been 'born with a silver spoon in his mouth' he was, over a period of time, able to acquire several sheep stations, and thus became a successful gentleman farmer. The next step was to enter politics and in 1854 he was elected to New Zealand's first Parliament. He served for two terms as the member for Waimea before being elected to the position of Speaker of the House, occupying that chair during six changes of government. He was knighted in 1866 and retired from politics in 1872.

Sir David's son Charles John was educated at Nelson College and was then sent to England to continue his studies at Christ College, Finchley. Whilst at Christ College he was also to learn a new sport — rugby football! In 1870 upon returning to New Zealand he was instrumental in getting his old school, Nelson College, to include the rugby code as one of their sports, and later he was a member of the team which played the first match between Nelson

and Wellington. After working for some time on various of his father's sheep stations, Charles then travelled overseas. While in Europe he furthered his studies, particularly in music. After returning to Nelson in 1885 he married a banker's daughter, Helena Beatrice MacDonald. Their two-year honeymoon was spent doing the grand tour of Europe and their first child, David, was born during this time.

During his earlier travelling in the North Island Charles had seen and fallen in love with some land sited on a plateau above a bush-clad escarpment that looked down over the Manawatu River to the growing township of Palmerston North. This area was known as Fitzherbert West. He purchased 51 acres upon which he wished to develop a garden and orchard, for he was a keen botanist and gardener and his career ambitions were more horticultural than pastoral. Whilst their grand two-storeyed house was being built the young family lived in Palmerston North, where a second son, John, was born. The new house was given the name Craiglockhart, which was the name of the Monro country estate in Scotland, and in 1890, shortly after they moved in, their daughter, Helen Mary, was born. The orchard, vegetable and flower gardens flourished in the very fertile Manawatu soil and by the time Linda Constance was born, in 1894, followed a year later by Peter, the gardens and orchard were well established and becoming quite famous for the varieties of plants, trees, vegetables and fruits that were growing so well. Being born into a well-to-do family where there were both inside servants and outside staff, Linda and Peter had a magical childhood. Peacocks strutted the formal garden area, a pink and grey galah was a household pet, and the six and a half acres of bush which was not cleared for cultivation was alive with native birds.

Being several years younger than their other siblings, Linda and Peter were bonded into a special companionship, which lasted all their lives. They spent hours playing in the bush where they had secret paths to special fairy glades, and in one of these mossy fern-decked dells lived an elusive little fairy called Angelina who would come to a special call. There were streams and a tinkling waterfall. They had many adventures both real and imagined, for there were also tigers and other fierce animals lurking in some dangerous parts of their fantasy world. When they returned from night-time eeling excursions the way through the bush was often lit by the twinkling lights of glow-worms hiding in their grottos in the banks. Although the older children had their first lessons from a governess, Linda and Peter had some of their early education from their father, followed by a brief spell at the Tiritea country school where their older brothers had also attended. At an appropriate age Peter was to join his brothers at boarding school in Wellington, and Linda became a member of the group of girls who daily rode down to Palmerston North to be educated at Craven School, an establishment run by three highly qualified sisters, the Misses Fraser.

There were several other wealthy families who had their mansions on this plateau area and there was much socialising among them all. They would ride out to special places along the river for picnics and swimming, and there were tennis, croquet, birthday and garden parties, lavish evening parties and dances with sumptuous champagne suppers, grand wedding receptions, concerts and music, roller skating and golf, as well as billiards and polo for the men. Each year, high on the calendar of events would be the Agricultural and Pastoral Show, which Linda's father had helped to establish.

The two eldest Monro sons went off to Edinburgh in 1905 and 1906 respectively to study medicine (in later years David also took up medical studies at Otago) and the exciting social life of the younger set continued. Then a shadow came down over Linda's life when in 1911, at the age of sixteen, she felt the first pains of rheumatoid arthritis. All the family were at home in 1912, the year that Mary married, and by then Linda's ailment was becoming much worse. An evil spell seemed to have been cast over the happy community on the hill as with the onset of the 1914–18 war one by one the young men went off to serve King and country and one of the girls from 'the set' also went to England to volunteer as a VAD (Voluntary Aid Detachment) then a WAAC (Womens Army Auxiliary Corps). For four years everything was tried to find a cure for Linda's cruel disease, with frequent trips to Rotorua for thermal treatment. She was even taken as far as Australia to seek a cure, without avail. It didn't matter how many members of the family were doctors: nobody had a cure to help her.

Fate had an even worse blow for this young woman who had led such a happy, active and athletic earlier life. In 1916, when she was in Rotorua

Hospital undergoing further treatment for her arthritis, there was an outbreak of poliomyelitis and poor Linda became a victim of this dreaded disease. She survived, spending two years at Rotorua before she was able to return to Craiglockhart as a wheelchair-bound paraplegic. The restriction of having to be wheeled about the house and flatter parts of the grounds must have been very difficult for such a high-spirited young woman, used to running free, swimming, riding and dancing. No longer could she

Some of the 1930s and 1940s cotton prints used in Linda Monro's quilt.

Linda Monro's very originally designed hexagon quilt using a wide variety of 1930s/1940s cotton prints. The top is lined and the layers are discreetly caught together with almost invisible stitches at counterpoints. 70¾" x 94"

scramble about the bush tracks to visit all the special and secret haunts of her childhood. However, Linda was blessed with a very sweet personality; everyone who knew her spoke in glowing terms of her gentle smiling face, and the happiness she seemed to generate created an aura about her that rubbed off on all who came within her ambit. She, like other members of her family, was accustomed to keeping diaries and journals, and Linda recorded in her journals everything that was happening, not only in beautiful descriptions of the changes in the garden, but also in reports on what was taking place both locally and in the world. She recorded many momentous events such as, in the 1920s, the sight of

the first aeroplanes to visit Palmerston North and the arrival of the 'movies' and, in the 1930s, the early radio-telephone calls between England, Australia and New Zealand. How she must have longed to be able to fly like those mechanical birds, and what inspiration she would have gained, for she knew it was coming, had she lived to see the flights to the moon that our generation have witnessed.

With the advent of the motor car and its growing use, Linda was able to be taken for drives and could more readily join in most of the outings her family and friends were attending. However her biggest joy came in 1946 when her family imported from England a battery-powered electric wheelchair thought to be the first of its type to come to New Zealand. She was elated at now regaining the freedom and, to a certain extent, independence to be able to travel into town and visit friends once more as the fancy took her and without having to rely so much on others for her transportation.

Linda wrote beautiful poetry and comic verse and, despite the handicap of the arthritis, was able to knit and embroider and was an accomplished painter. She painted tapestry pictures for friends to sew, and received great acclaim for, in particular, a tiny picture she delicately embroidered and which, at first glance, looked like an etching. This small gem was embroidered on silk and used as thread single strands of hair in gold, white and black; it depicted a little girl and her dog sitting on the side of a hill near a clump of silver birch trees. The girl was looking down the slope towards a thatched cottage and one wonders if, while she was sewing, Linda was seeing herself as that little girl and remembering her happy childhood before she was confined to looking down from the sunny veranda of Craiglockhart at the comings and goings of the farms and town below.

It is of course because Linda made a patchwork quilt that she is featured in this book. Linda's quilt (70¾" by 94") is made of hexagons (2 point to point) pieced over papers in the English method and the cottons used are a wonderful array of 1930s and 1940s prints. There is no batting but the two layers have been caught together, here and there, with discreetly placed almost invisible stitches, like a tied quilt. It was made over a period of time and completed in about 1954. The overall design is unique and beautiful, just what one would have expected of this delightful woman. The quilt has the appearance of a Persian carpet, and as it has not been used, it is as bright and fresh as the day it was completed. One wonders how Linda was able to assemble the components and put them so precisely into the complicated pattern when she was confined to a wheelchair. Linda's niece Mrs Joan Moore (Mary's daughter) inherited this lovely piece of work and it will later be passed on to her granddaughter.

In the late 1920s an agricultural college was established in the Fitzherbert Road area and as it grew into what was later to become Massey University, one by one the lovely old mansions on the plateau were gradually acquired to become part of the campus. When Joan Gaisford married John Gifford Moore in 1940 she was the last bride to be married from Craiglockhart before it too was absorbed by the university, to become a hostel for women. With its change of ownership, along with the other mansions acquired by the university, it also lost its name and is now known as Moginie House.

Linda, together with her mother and sister, took up residence in Fitzherbert Avenue. Mrs Helena Monro died in 1962 at the grand old age of 97, and Linda, aged 69, the following year.

The Mackereth Quilt (circa 1730s)

The lawless state of England after the unsuccessful Jacobean rebellion made travelling around the countryside a dangerous undertaking. Squire Arthur Mackereth, a large landowner in the Lake District who knew more roads and paths than the roaming highwaymen, was entrusted to take a large shipment of gold bullion from Lancaster to Carlisle, a very risky task in those very lawless times. With the mission accomplished he was presented with a beautiful china tea and coffee service. It was handcrafted and reputed to be one of only two sets made. The cups, as was common then, did not have handles. This must have been a very substantial gift of appreciation, for nearly 200 years after the presentation the set was officially valued at more than £40,000 sterling. Several years prior to the signing of the 1840 Treaty of Waitangi which established British sovereignty over New Zealand, a branch of the Mackereth family had become early settlers in Northland. One of Arthur Mackereth's descendants, also called Arthur Mackereth, while on leave from France during World War I visited the old family home at Ambleside on the shores of Windermere. He explored this beautiful region of Cumbria and in the little church at Troutbeck near Ambleside found records that his family had lived in the area since the fifteenth century. The old home has since been pulled down and the only part of it to survive is a balustrade, which now adorns a local youth hostel.

In 1902 the famous tea and coffee service was split up and distributed amongst the many great-grandsons of the original Arthur Mackereth. Some years after World War I several pieces of the service were brought to New Zealand, along with other items from the old Westmoreland family home. These included a patchwork quilt made by the squire's daughters in, it is believed, 1731, and a handsome adzed and pegged oak chest bearing the inscription A.M. 1709.

The quilt measures 81″ x 74″ and is made with 1½″ cotton squares with borders of three different widths, 1¾″, 2″, and 3¾″. Triangles form the 1¾″ wide border, which is then followed by two wider borders pieced from various pieces of cotton prints and plaids, with a four-patch pattern forming in each corner. A multitude of very interesting prints has been used, some of them different colour breaks of the same design, one of which pictures tiny centaurs. The fineness of this particular print and the type of printing used indicates the quilt would have been made in the eighteenth century, possibly around 1731 — or perhaps it was started in that year and completed later. One of the prettiest prints is of a rose with leaf sprays and buds which has unfortunately faded to give only a shadow of its original beauty. The placement of the darker 1½″ squares gives the impression of this being a traditional medallion design.

The batting appears to be a hand-woven woollen blanket and the lining is linen. One corner of the linen has been repaired with a linen of lesser quality which is clearly of more recent vintage as it has some machine sewing on the hem, and the quilting is inferior to the rest of the quilt, done at the time of the repair by a less skilled quilter. There is quite a lot of water staining on the lining.

Apart from the repaired area the rest of the quilt is hand-stitched and hand quilted in a chevron pattern — not very small stitches. There is no binding, the top being turned to the back and hemmed down. On the back, close to the edge and partly obscured by this hem, in tiny red cross-stitching are the initials A:W with an R below the A. Possibly these are the initials of the daughters who, it is believed, made the quilt for the adventurous Squire Arthur Mackereth.

Many of the cottons used have retained their colours very well, though parts of the quilt which have obviously been exposed to sunlight through a window have faded badly. Although some of the fabrics have started to deteriorate, for its age the quilt is in good order.

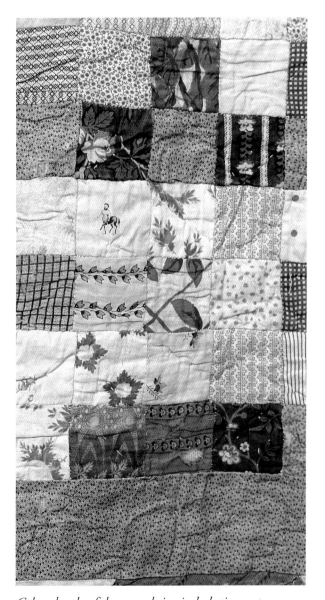

Colour breaks of the same design include tiny centaurs.

*A cotton quilt with hand-woven woollen batting and linen lining, made circa 1731 in Westmoreland ,
England by Squire Arthur Mackereth's three daughters. 81″ x 74″*

Mary McLean Patterson (1858–1943)

Little is known of the woman who was always referred to as Granny Patterson in her later life, as she was at all times very secretive about her origins. She came from Tasmania and was born in either 1858 or 1859, a date too late to indicate that she had arrived on one of the convict ships, but she could possibly have been the daughter of convicts. Mary married three times; McLean is believed to have been her second husband's name. She had a physically handicapped daughter Constance, from her first marriage, who lived all her life in Tasmania. From the second marriage there were two children, Maggie and Jim, who were subsequently adopted by her third husband, Cornelius M. Patterson, a Canadian. He had been a construction worker on the Panama Canal, but his main occupation was mining in California, the Yukon and Australia until the call of gold fever saw Cornelius and family cross the Tasman to try their luck at the Thames goldfields. The family later took up farming in the Ormond area of Gisborne. As well as being a fine needlewoman, Mary was also a keen gardener and every inch of the ground up to the cottage door was planted with vegetables and flowers. She was also a charlady, walking into Gisborne to clean the Bank of New South Wales premises as well as private homes. The ladies of the houses she cleaned may also have been the source of supply of some of the luxury fabric scraps she used in her quiltmaking. Mary can best be described in the words of her grandson's wife, June MacGibbon:

A 'tough old girl' is how my husband remembers her. Married to Cornelius Patterson, her third husband, at an age that she thought would be too old to procreate she found that she had made a mistake and my mother-in-law, Alma, was the result. Hence the tale that Cornelius was banished to an outhouse. He did not actually meet Hone Heke but was one of a vigilante group ready and willing to ride out if and when he came to Ormond.

Granny Patterson lived at Ormond, a short distance out of Gisborne, in a small cottage and all her life cooked over an open fire. My husband remembers her as having the texture and smell of a smoked fish. Her quilting and exquisite needlework were done by candlelight right up to the end of her life. As well as quilting and sewing she was a fantastic gardener and not an inch of her section was uncultivated.

She had her first ride in a car in about 1935. It was her last as she gave that away. It was no good to her. She went to Napier to see about cataracts, but nothing was done and she refused to go away again or shift. About that time, and at the age of 85, she was attacked one night and brutally beaten, but put up such a fight that the police easily picked up her assailant by the brands she put on him. However she died not long after, probably as a result. Several of her quilts were burnt when her property was cleaned out.

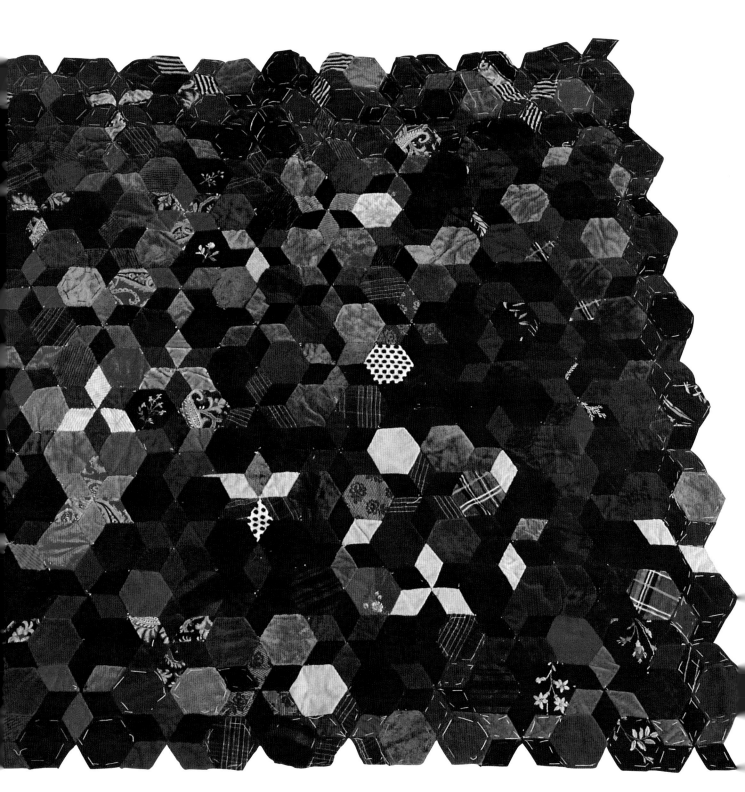

One of the incomplete paper pieced quilt tops made by Granny Patterson, dated on one paper template at 1908.

Detail of a section of Granny Patterson's quilt top showing embroidered embellishments and tacking stitches.

Mr MacGibbon also recalls that Granny Patterson had teeth like a horse and wore long black dresses, and he remembers that all the beds always had quilts on them.

Sadly, Granny Patterson in her anger at Cornelius tended to give her youngest daughter rather a hard time, but she idolised Alma's son (Mr MacGibbon).

He inherited the remaining two incomplete quilts, one of which (58⅝″ by 75¼″) would have been a very handsome quilt if finished, as it is pieced mainly from rich glowing colours of plain printed, tufted, corded, sculptured and striped velvets and brocades. Diamond shapes (11¼″ by 2⅛″) are formed into six-point stars surrounded by hexagons (2¼″ sides by 2½″ width and length) which interlock into a mosaic allover design with the stars predominating. On eleven of the black hexagon or diamond shapes Mary has embroidered in silks of red, pink, gold, yellow, cream, green, blue and lavender scattered sprays of flowers and leaves. As with so many of the old quilts remaining in New Zealand, Mary used the technique of tacking her fabrics over paper templates; one of the remaining papers in this piece of work has the date 1908 recorded on it.

The other surviving unfinished quilt is the same design but is constructed from a wide variety of coloured printed cottons with pinks and reds predominating. This is a very interesting piece of work because of the papers still left in it. They are school sums and writing lessons, accounts, magazine pages and so on. One paper has the date 1896 printed on it. Although Granny Patterson obviously had a colourful and somewhat hard life, she had received a reasonable education and had been instructed in the gentle art of needlework, and therefore made sure her children also had the benefit of a good education.

The Spencer Family Quilt

Dora Green was born in 1871 and lived at her family home, Holywell, near Claverdon in Warwickshire, England, until she was sixteen, when her much-loved mother died. As her father was frequently away from home on business, Dora and her three half sisters decided to become governesses, and she spent the next five years in this occupation. During this time she became engaged to Samuel King Spencer, whose parents and Dora's had been friends of long standing. The Spencers, also of Warwickshire, had been farmers since the twelfth century, first at Snitterfield then Wormleighton. The original de Spencer had come to England as part of William the Conqueror's supporters, the name being recorded on the gates at Battle Abbey near Hastings. The Snitterfield land was understood to have been a grant from William for services rendered during the conquest.

In 1893 King emigrated to New Zealand in order to acquire land to begin farming and set up a home for his bride to be. His first venture was to buy a small orchard on the banks of the Clive River, in Hawke's Bay. It had a pleasant little home with a beautiful garden which he knew would appeal to Dora, and he promptly named the property Holywell. This venture was brought to a disastrous end when a flood occurred which ruined the house and the property. He then travelled north to Gisborne, where land was cheaper, and so as to nurture the remains of his money he took a seven-year lease of a property which

had a small cottage on it with furniture which he was able to purchase. The land was poor but he was prepared to work hard to clear, sow, fence and stock the property.

Once he was sufficiently established and beginning to make ends meet, King felt it was time for Dora to join him, so on 21 January 1897 she departed England on the RMS *Tongariro*. Most of her luggage had been shipped ahead of her, including some of her mother's beautiful needlework, her tapestry chair and a fine collection of china her mother had inherited from an uncle who had died in 1829. Also included in Dora's luggage was a patchwork bedcover which is believed to have been made circa 1845 by Misses Emily and Anne Green, maiden aunts of Penelope Green, Dora's mother. Upon her mother's death, Dora inherited this lovely old bedspread.

A huge variety of cotton prints has been used in what appears at first glance to be a mosaic design, but on closer examination six-point stars in two sizes are revealed, each star having a small hexagon in the centre. With the addition of triangle shapes between the points of the stars, hexagons are formed. Using colours as a guide, sets of the stars have been skilfully arranged in patterns that are almost hidden when the cover is on a bed, but nicely revealed when it is displayed as a hanging. A circle of tiny stars in the centre is flanked on either side by pairs of larger stars, and semicircles of three large red stars curve above and below this central area. The remainder of the stars form other borders developed both by their sizes and colours until they reach a border of two rows of multicoloured squares framing the whole. Finally there is a wide muted yellow border with pale pink squares in each corner. The ladies who stitched this work had a fine sense of design and colour.

King and Dora worked very hard on the leasehold property, clearing the land, sowing seed, stocking it and bringing it into production. However, in 1900, two years before the lease period was up, the next door farmer — who had previously unsuccessfully tried to work this piece of land for the absentee owners, but who had nevertheless been appointed their agent — was able to convince the owners that the property wasn't being farmed to the terms of the lease. This wasn't in fact true; nevertheless, they were forced to surrender the lease without compensation for the improvements they had made, and the stock was taken over at valuation. They had been relying on two more years of improved stock returns, larger wool cheques and some compensation for their hard toil to enable them to seek out another property to purchase. They had been forced to pay a full year's rent on the farm, but were required to leave the property in May, with no refund for the portion of the year's rent remaining. Needless to say the agent was subsequently able to buy in the much-improved farm for a song.

Winter was not the best of times to be undertaking such an upheaval, which added to their disappointment. By this time they had a son under the age of two and a new little baby daughter who had been born in January. King located a 260-hectare freehold property over 150 kilometres away at Tauwhareparae, in the Tolaga Bay area. It had some bush and was mostly unimproved. It also had the disadvantage of having a considerable area of manuka and fern, which they had hoped to have seen the last of at the recently vacated farm. However, besides the fact that it was freehold, it also had the advantage of having a new house, and at a distance from this dwelling there was also a cottage.

After the exhausting task of packing up their belongings (which had to be done with some skill as most of the transportation would be by packhorse) and arranging for them to be sent to Tolaga Bay, the young couple faced the gruelling journey from Gisborne to their new home. Dora and the two babies were to travel by the public coach and King followed on horseback, leading his wife's mare. The day was cold and stormy and much of the journey was along the beach, which in some places had treacherous reefs that had to be negotiated while the tide was low. With the wind blowing through the flapping side-curtains and the coach rocking and lurching, the young mother had to clutch the children to her for most of the day to keep them

Cotton coverlet made circa 1845 near Claverdon, Warwickshire, England by Misses Emily & Anne Green, great-aunts of Dora Spencer who brought it to New Zealand in 1897. It is now at Gisborne Museum and Art Centre. 105" x 105"

Detail of design elements in the Spencer family quilt.

warm and prevent them from tumbling off the seats. Sometimes the horses were splashing their way through the surf, which had been whipped into huge crashing waves. It was almost dark before they were able to leave the beaches and continue the rest of the journey on the muddy track that was the 'road'. The coach and its tired horses then had to crawl up and over the steep Tolaga Bay hill and be transported across the Uawa River by punt before they reached the township of Tolaga Bay and the warmth, food and comfort of the hotel.

Even after this dreadful, exhausting journey, the next day the couple set off, each carrying a child in front of them, to ride the remaining 45 kilometres — a distance that would take them two days — to Tauwhareparae. A kindly neighbour who had offered them overnight accommodation invited Dora and the children to stay on until King could bring their belongings by packhorse from Tolaga Bay. The weather was dreadful; with continuous rain for three weeks, the roads and tracks were a sea of mud, putting dreadful strain on both the young farmer and the packhorses. After the three weeks' respite and with sufficient of their belongings and supplies already at the house, Dora was feeling strong enough to move to their new home and set about unpacking and making it comfortable.

The inclement weather had not only posed problems for the packing in of their personal effects and equipment, it also meant that the house was not yet complete. There was no stove, the water tank had not arrived, and it had not been wise for a lot of their nice furniture to be brought in. Dora had to learn how to cook their meagre food supplies in camp ovens and the water had to be brought by bucket from a nearby creek. King had to find time to chop a constant supply of firewood, a chore that used up valuable hours he could better have utilised on his farming work. On the bright side was the amount of space they had — a roomy kitchen, living-room and three bedrooms. They brought over from the farm cottage some kitchen chairs and a table, and converted the packing cases into clothes chests. The lovely patchwork bedspread was also put to use as a doorway curtain until the house interior was completed. They had a few scrawny chickens, which laid fitfully, and a house cow that, due to the scarcity of good fodder, was able to provide only about a quart of milk per day. Wild pigs provided much of their meat, and their hospitable neighbour generously provided them with butter when she had some to spare. As the weather improved so did the health of their animals as more food became available for them; the farm work was able to progress, a vegetable garden and orchard were promptly planted, and later a flower garden.

The Spencers successfully farmed their property through good times and bad, adding more land when it became available and leasing some until they were eventually farming over 10,000 acres. They employed many local Maori families as well as other New Zealanders and up until the beginning of World War I always had a string of young English farm cadets working and training on the land. No fewer than six of these young Englishmen enlisted for that war on the same day, one eventually returning to claim the eldest Spencer daughter as his bride.

The Spencers had three daughters and three sons, all of whom had to be sent to boarding school for their education after first having their early learning from governesses, and they all returned to help run the expanding farming enterprise. At one stage the house they first moved into was dismantled and moved to another site, at which time it also had more rooms added on. King died in 1934 and the family continued to run the various farms. Dora and her two younger daughters finally left The Homestead in 1951 to move into Gisborne, where Dora died in 1961.

The family, either at the time of departing from the farm or after Dora's death, donated this lovely bedcover to the Gisborne Museum and Arts Centre, which has a small collection of old quilts that are well worth a visit.

Jane Tryon (née Philips, 1792–?)

Mrs Patsy Armstrong of Auckland is the proud current owner of a Grandmother's Flower Garden quilt made circa 1810 by her great-great-great-grandmother, Jane Philips, born in Wales in 1792.

Miles Philips was the son of a wealthy merchant of Pontypool, a seaport town in Monmouthshire, Wales. When he was a young man he attended a Baptist convention as a lay delegate and was billeted with a leading member of the church, a Mr Evans. Mr and Mrs Evans had one child, Margaret, who was not only a great heiress but also very beautiful. It was love at first sight. Miles was very handsome and wore a powdered queue (pigtail), a sure sign of a gentleman of position and means, for at that time a heavy tax was levied on the powder used for dressing the coiffure of a wealthy, fashionable lady or gentleman.

After they were married they lived at his country estate, Beulah, in a large beautiful house surrounded by tenanted farms, and had a full complement of servants — maids, nurses, cook, coachman, footman and so on — to care for them and their increasing family. However, with the onset of the Napoleonic wars and the fear of an invasion by the French, Mrs Philips became very alarmed, doubtless recalling what had happened to titled and wealthy aristocrats during the recent revolution across the channel. Apparently, with all England and Wales in excited fear of Napoleon and his troops landing on their shores, the Welsh women donned their red cloaks and paraded up and down the paths along the cliffs. They did this to give the impression that they were British redcoat soldiers guarding the coast, and thus help deter French ships from debarking any invasion troops they might be transporting. This security measure didn't satisfy Margaret Philips; finally, she managed to persuade her husband, against his judgement, to exchange his beautiful estate for one in America, which he unwisely purchased from a map. At her solicitation he took up all her property and that of their seven children, who each had a separate portion, and in 1798, with all their possessions, plus their large retinue of servants, they sailed to America.

Arriving in the promised land they soon found that they had been duped, for the non-existent estate they had purchased was in fact on the top of the Allegheny Mountains. Things went from bad to worse, for whatever he did to try to retrieve the investment failed. Admitting defeat, he gathered together what was left of his money, and the family left New York for Philadelphia, where he was reduced to becoming a clerk in an insurance office.

The eldest daughter, Anne, married shortly after arriving in America but was lost at sea en route for Savannah, Georgia. Jane and her younger sister Mary were 'adopted' by a cousin of Mrs Philips, Ruth Probyn, who was married to a very wealthy merchant of Welsh birth, and went to live with Mr and Mrs Edward Probyn in their fine large house in New York city. It was customary and more respectful for young people to call older members of their family uncle and aunt, even though they were really second cousins. In 1808, when Jane was sixteen years old, uncle Edward wished her to marry a Baptist minister, the Reverend Charles Mays, but the high-spirited Jane had already fallen in love with another handsome gentleman of good birth, William Tryon, so they promptly eloped — and at the same time the Reverend Mays eloped with Jane's fourteen-year-old sister, Mary. The two young couples must have been forgiven, for some years later another of the Philips' daughters married Marshall Tryon, a brother of Jane's husband, and they all remained closely connected to the Probyns as part of their family.

The fine old quilt which has come down to Mrs Armstrong was made by Jane using the English paper piecing method while she was travelling in a covered wagon-train heading west from New York. Jane and William were happy in their marriage and produced four children, but the last one, Margaret, was born on 2 January 1821 after her father had 'died in St Louis on the Astor Expedition to the Far West in 1820'. This information is taken from family documents, but no indication is given as to what the expedition was for (probably land acquisition), nor why William had died at the relatively young age of 36. Jane and her family returned to New York to the Probyns', where she presumably remained until her death. No

date of death is recorded in family papers, but she was numbered amongst those who went with Mr Probyn to view the *Great Western*, the first passenger steamer to cross the ocean, on its arrival after its maiden voyage to America in 1838. Jane's granddaughter Ida Eliot recorded her memories of her grandmother in later life as 'a tall, erect, handsome woman of great dignity and imposing appearance'.

After Jane's death her youngest daughter, Margaret, inherited the quilt and it has subsequently been handed down to the eldest daughter or granddaughter through each generation. Jane's great-granddaughter Ida Margaret Summerfield was born on 7 January 1886 at Flatbush, Long Island, New York, and in 1915 travelled to Wales, arriving by train at Pontypool from whence her ancestors Miles and Margaret Philips and their family had departed in 1801. On 7 April 1915 she was married to Welshman Bwenard William Harris Pratt. This was at the height of World War I, so she returned to the United States while her husband was serving in the army in Salonika. Possibly she returned to her family for the birth of their daughter Margaret Eliot (Peggy) Pratt, born on 11 December 1916 at Philadelphia. Peggy (Patsy Armstrong's mother) married Vincent O. Harvey in England in 1940, and Patsy was born on 9 February 1948 at Ardleigh, Colchester. When Patsy was two years old the Harveys emigrated to New Zealand.

Cotton hexagon Grandmother's Flower Garden hand pieced circa 1809 by Jane Philips Tryon while travelling west from New York City in a covered wagon train. 91" x 98½"

Detail of hexagons and the border triangles of Jane Tryon's quilt.

Patsy married Francis Charles Armstrong in 1968. In 1956 Margaret Pratt, following the death of her husband, came to this country to live with her daughter Peggy Harvey at Whangaroa Harbour until her death. She brought the well-travelled quilt with her to hand on to Peggy, and when Peggy passed away in 1977 it was time for Patricia Margaret Armstrong to inherit her great-great-great-grandmother's quilt. It will remain in her keeping and will be passed on to her daughter Leanne Margaret Armstrong or her first granddaughter by Leanne.

This grand old quilt measures 91″ by 98½″ and comprises 63 hexagon flowers and 36 half-flowers, with 86 coloured triangles forming the border. The hexagons are 2⅞″ wide and form flowers of 5⅝″ in diameter, and the triangles are 4″ across the base and

4¾″ tall. A wide variety of coloured cottons was used, in solids, stripes, prints, checks, polka dots, etc. Some of the fabrics are shirting and ribbed cottons, and in several places the hexagons or border triangles have had the fabric skilfully pieced to give sufficient material to cut the required shape. The flowers have been nicely placed with regard to their colours and in the central area a group of flowers in dark colours almost form a diamond-shaped medallion. There is no batting. The whole top is quilted around each flower and each border triangle, and there are two rows of quilting around the whole edge of the quilt. The quilting stitches are even and there seem to be eight to twelve stitches per inch. For its age the quilt is in good order, with very little fading and a minimal amount of damage, which has been carefully repaired.

Appliqué, Broderie Perse & Embroidered Quilts

Some lovers of old quilts believe that the origin of the term appliqué (past participle of the French verb *appliquer,* to apply) in relation to quilts originally referred to a patch applied to repair a worn or torn part. This use of the word certainly helps to illustrate the differences between pieced, paper piecing and whole-cloth patchwork techniques, but though it may have originally been associated with old, much-repaired, patched quilts, the appliqué technique soon took on a whole new character for the expert needlewoman.

Ardent quiltmakers seem for several centuries to have aspired to make at least one appliqué quilt in their sewing careers as it enabled them to create in picture form the beauty, especially floral, they saw about them in their daily lives, and to commemorate special occasions. Many who became experts in this form of needlework forsook the other techniques to devote their time to making only appliqué quilts. The women who stitched with invisible stitches the glorious Baltimore album quilts, for example, used many pieces of fabric, plain and printed, to create their beautiful multicoloured designs. The needlewomen of Hawaii, for another example, made dramatic statements by the use of two plain colours, usually Turkey red on white to begin with, then enhanced the coverlets with rows and rows of echo quilting (where the lines of quilting echo the shape of the appliqué for row after row). Missionary wives introduced Hawaiian women to patchwork and quilting in the first quarter of the nineteenth century; and as Hawaiian school students were probably also taught how to create a repeating pattern by folding paper and then cutting out a design, their mothers and aunts no doubt thought this would be a splendid way to create their own dramatic appliqué designs. Like their quilting sisters throughout the world, these women illustrated in fabric the flowers and trees they saw in their gardens and forests, and thus created another very distinct patchwork style.

With the opening up of trade with India, English needlewomen found another source of materials in the seventeenth and eighteenth centuries: palampore — Indian bedcovers with resplendent and exotic

Persian and oriental designs printed or painted on cotton cloth known as chints (the original name for the particoloured printed cottons we now know as chintz). As with all new items to come from faraway places, these textiles, whether in the form of a bedspread or a length of fabric, were at first far too expensive to use for anything as ordinary as a domestic bedcover except for the very wealthy. However, palampore eventually dropped in price and was found in more and more homes. When it later began to wear out, the thrifty needlewomen were able to salvage the exotic birds, flowers, fruits and trees depicted in the colourful designs and appliqué them onto plain fabric backgrounds.

Some skilled needlewomen still appliquéd the cut-out pieces by turning their edges under in the accustomed way. Many, however, used buttonhole stitch instead, so that they would not need to turn under edges that could include many sharp corners, either inwards or outwards, and other complicated and intricate areas. By leaving the edges raw and closely buttonhole stitching around the patch they not only simplified and speeded up the sewing but also strengthened the edges and possibly circumvented the fraying out of sharp points. By the middle of the nineteenth century this form of appliqué had acquired the name broderie perse. No doubt the fashionable needlewoman felt this French name (meaning Persian embroidery) added to the

appeal of the often delicate, and certainly exotic, fabric she had used in making her quilt.

The quilts were often made in medallion form with a central appliquéd square surrounded by a combination of pieced and appliquéd borders, or blocks. Some had a central broderie perse medallion and corner appliqués, with other broderie perse pieces scattered around the medallion, and often these quilts were intricately quilted, sometimes with parts of the quilting stuffed to raise these areas and add more character and beauty to the design. The appliquéd central medallion, be it square, round or oval, continued to be very popular, so by the early nineteenth century manufacturers began to market especially-produced panels using all the favourite motifs of birds and butterflies, trees, fruits and flowers in various forms — bunches, wreaths, branches, baskets and urns.

See page 100, for the Black sisters' broderie perse quilt with appliquéd shells; page 111 for Anne Romsey's quilt with the palampore broderie perse centre with pheasants and broderie perse corner flowers; and page 114 for Miss McClure's quilt with a specially printed medallion and broderie perse appliqués.

Girls in past centuries were taught from an early age not only to sew a straight seam but also to be accomplished embroiderers. Often one of the first articles they completed, once they were able to manipulate a needle well, would be a sampler, which would frequently have an embroidered alphabet and rows of the various embroidery stitches they had learned to sew. They would also embroider their name and either the date the work was completed or, perhaps, their birth date. In more affluent homes where the young women were perhaps not called upon to do menial work about the home, their education could sometimes include a study of botany. They would collect flowers and leaves, perhaps just to press and put into albums, but those who had drawing masters or governesses would also sketch and paint the flowers they gathered. These flowers could also be the source of a design for their embroideries. Although old embroidered-only quilts are rarely seen in New Zealand, the Canterbury Museum has two fine examples in their collection: Sarah White (née Sandcraft) pages 104–105, and Lettice Oldfield, below and pages 102–103 embroidered their quilts in 1743 and 1707 respectively.

An embroidered bedcover by Lettice Oldfield showing her wonderful precision quilting.

Francis Cleland

The Cleland quilt, part of the fine collection of quilts at Broadgreen House in Nelson, was thought for some time to be the oldest in New Zealand, but it is predated by the privately owned Mackereth quilt (page 81) and by two embroidered quilts in the Canterbury Museum collection, one by Lettice Oldfield (page 102) and the other by Sarah White (page 104). The quilt at Broadgreen belonged to Mrs Francis Cleland, a member of the family that went from Scotland to Ireland in

1703–4 and built Stormont Castle in Belfast, and which is credited with starting the first Church of Ireland Sunday School in Ireland.

In 1746 Francis wove the white linen background fabric that she used to create and line her pieced and appliquéd coverlet. This may have been a wedding quilt, as the central area has a scattered design of appliquéd hearts, circles and stars and one of the borders also features hearts and stars. The quilt is 86½″ by 90¼″ in

The central medallion portion of Francis Cleland's quilt, which is part of the quilt collection at Broadgreen House, Nelson.

size, the central square being 31 1/4″ by 32 3/4″. This is surrounded by a border of 2 3/4″ squares on point, then another wider border of appliquéd eight-point stars cut in one piece alternating between sets of four hearts appliquéd to form a flower or perhaps a stylised shamrock, as this particular fabric, which is now light brown, is thought to have faded from its original green.

These two borders are edged on all sides by strips gradually increasing in width. Up to this stage all the motifs and edges have been cut from the same piece of navy blue print. The next border is made up of

Detail of another part of the Francis Cleland quilt.

A corner of the same quilt showing five of the nine borders used to frame the central medallion.

diamonds on point in muted coloured prints of cotton shirting or chintz, mainly with scattered flowers on a cream background, each diamond being edged with a narrow strip in various complementary floral prints with a fair representation of pale blue and the occasional appearance of the navy blue used in the main area. There are larger eight-point stars cut in one piece in each corner. The next border comprises half-square triangles pieced in the sawtooth pattern, the top and bottom borders being in a taupe print and the two sides in a print of pale blue, cream and pale brown in a wavy line pattern. The taupe is then used for the next plain border on either side with a paler print on the ends. The final border utilises a further print on three sides and strip piecing in two prints on the fourth. There is no batting but the cover is entirely quilted in a chevron (zigzag) pattern.

One of the prints in this quilt is similar, if not identical, to one used in a quilt seen in the Otago Museum, made in Edinburgh in the mid–1770s. One wonders if the two women who made these quilts knew each other and exchanged fabrics as patchworker friends do, or perhaps they just purchased what may have been a popular print of the day from the same shop. Nevertheless, it is a wonderful coincidence that two very old quilts which originated in fairly close proximity to each other should still be in existence, in good fettle, right across the other side of the world, being lovingly cared for just a few hundred miles away from each other.

Elizabeth Corne (née Black, circa 1774–1845) & Maria Black (circa 1774–1855)

These two sisters were born around 1774 in County Armagh, Northern Ireland, and spent most of their lives in Belfast. Mrs Corne, whose husband was an academician, died in 1845 and her unwed sister, Maria, in 1855. They had a younger sister, Martha Alicia, who was born in 1776 and died in 1815. Prior to Martha's marriage to Charles Brett the two sisters made for her, between 1790 and 1793, a handsome broderie perse quilt. It measures 82½" x 77¾", and comprises a central 24" square of white linen appliquéd with a basket of flowers surrounded by four floral swags and floral motifs in each corner.

Broderie perse wedding quilt made in 1790–93 in County Armagh, Northern Ireland. 82½" x 77¾"

'Clamshell' was a shape often used by skilled needlewomen in their appliqués and as a quilting pattern.

Broderie perse appliqué using buttonhole stitch to attach the pieces as well as to emphasise certain features.

Buttonhole stitch in coarse silk has been used to appliqué this medallion and all the other pictorial motifs. The square is surrounded by a 5″ tan border edged on each side with 2″ narrow printed borders. The tan area is appliquéd with clamshell-shaped chintz prints using hidden stitches, not buttonhole stitching. A 9½″ linen border follows, with sixteen broderie perse appliqués spaced around the medallion. These depict an urn and two baskets of flowers; bouquets; and little scenes, some of them depicting Chinese pagodas and trees, and two of them, little figures, each standing under a tree, and with one of the figures holding a parasol. One lavish display of flowers also has an exotic pheasant perched on a branch. The buttonhole stitch in some places has been used to create stems or branches and, in one area, a pair of flowers — which might indicate that the ladies ran out of chintz and used this method to balance the block. Straight stitching and French knots have also been used to embellish some flowers. The top is finished off with a further tan border with appliquéd clamshells and narrow strip edges of yet two more fancy prints. There is a linen backing, and though there is no batting, the two layers are held together with quilting in a zigzag pattern which is also known as chevron or Van Dyke pattern.

Martha and Charles passed the quilt on to their youngest son, Wills Hill Brett (1798–1862), who married Martha Matilda Garrett (1809–86). They in turn gave the quilt to their daughter Martha Alicia Brett when she came to New Zealand to marry George Hill Mackisack. Martha Alicia Mackisack passed the quilt to her daughter Martha Brett Mackisack, probably at the time of her marriage to Thomas Bolton Arlidge in 1908. She, in turn, handed the quilt on to her daughter Mary Alicia Jones in 1970. Mrs Jones is going to hand the quilt on to her daughter, who also has a daughter to inherit this treasure after her.

The quilt is in extremely good condition for its age, with minimal deterioration to only two of the fabrics and virtually no fading, a great indication of the loving care which each generation has given this lovely old quilt.

Lettice Oldfield

Little is known of Lettice Oldfield, who lived the bulk of her life at Oldfield Lawn, Sussex. Presumably this is the name of the family home, as it does not appear as a town or village on current maps. Thomas Oldfield (1845–1902) arrived in New Zealand from Sussex and settled in Taranaki. He was a member of the Armed Constabulary from 1864 to 1866 at the time of the land wars. The quilt belonged to his family, and Mrs G. Grant, his granddaughter, presented it to the Canterbury Museum.

Lettice embroidered the four cream linen panels which make up the main part of this quilt and signed it in the top right-hand corner 'Oldfield 1707'. The four pieces are believed to have been joined together around the 1780s or 1790s, possibly to make a marriage coverlet, and at the same time the 10¼″ wide border was added.

The cotton fabric used for the border is of a typical eighteenth-century neo-classical design printed in yellow ochre and brown on a cream background. Portions of this print have also been used to form an eight-pointed 'flower' in the centre of the top, covering the point where the four panels are joined to disguise and minimise the fact that the panels do not really match up. Two of the outer corners do not have the border print but each has a square of a coarser cream linen (not as fine as the linen used for the embroidered panels). The top is also lined with this linen. Often this technique of a plain square on the two corners at the foot of the bed was used where the quilt had to be tucked down around the bed posts and thus would tend to wear out long before the rest of the quilt did. The overall size of the quilt is 78½″ wide by 88¾″ long.

Border prints used by Lettice Oldfield to complete her quilt.

Lettice embroidered the four panels with sprays of flowers and leaves using three shades of green, the lights of which are almost yellow, plus pink, cream and crimson. All the embroideries have been worked using a tiny chain stitch so exact that one could have thought one of the early sewing machines had been used, but this boon to needlewomen throughout the world had not at this stage been invented.

All the cream background has been quilted in pale yellow in the clamshell pattern using backstitch.

Embroidered quilt made by Lettice Oldfield in 1707. The inset shows the amazingly accurate clamshell quilting which covers the whole quilt. 78½" x 88¾"

Sarah White (née Sandcraft)

The Sandcraft family lived at Wingham, near Canterbury in Kent, and were possibly fairly wealthy, as their daughter Sarah would appear to have been well educated in the gentle arts of fine needlework and painting and obviously had an interest in botany. No record is available to indicate when she was born or when she died. She was married to Thomas White, a sea captain who was involved with the Iceland fisheries industry. They lived at St Peter's, near Broadstairs, Kent, and produced eight children — Stephen born 1743, Catherine 1746, Mary 1749, Sarah 1752, John 1754, Thomas 1757, Isaac 1761, and Lydia, the youngest, who was born in 1764 and died in 1858. Lydia inherited the quilt made by her mother. From the fairly regular spacing of three to four years between the births of these children we could speculate that possibly the captain was away from home for several years at a time, as was often the norm for seafarers in the days of sail. With a fairly large brood of children and a sea captain for a husband, Sarah would probably have had household servants. This would have enabled her to have time to continue with her beautiful embroidery and artistic interests.

A descendant living in Massachusetts has inherited an album with hundreds of flowers hand painted by Sarah White, and descendants living in New Zealand have gifted to the Canterbury Museum in Christchurch a sampler made by Sarah in 1754 and a table napkin dated 1750. But the most impressive example of her work donated by these family members is a beautiful hand-embroidered quilt.

Embroidered quilt made by Sarah White in 1743, with details above and left. Pairs of circles were used as a quilting design in the central area and the 'Wineglass' design for the rest of the main part of the quilt. The borders are quilted with leaf shapes. 87¼" x 94½"

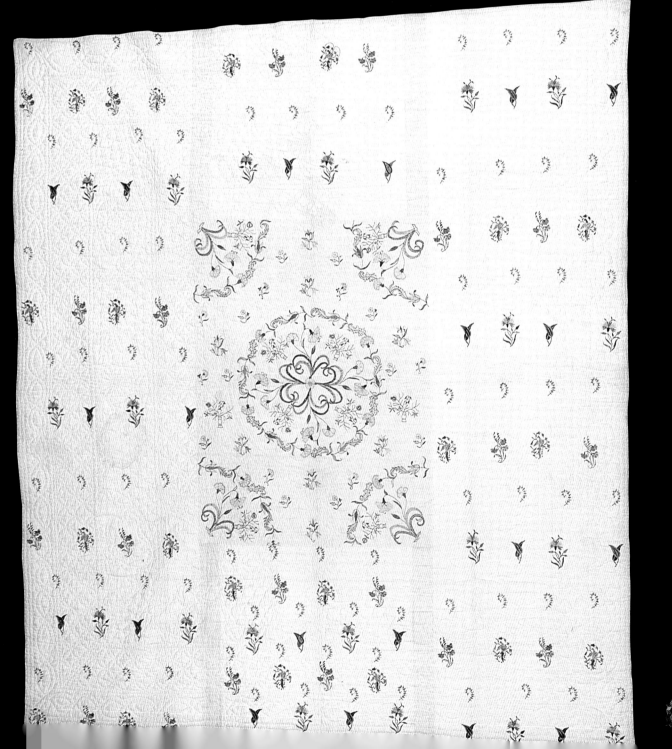

Sarah's quilt has an inscription on the lining: 'Worked in the year 1743 by Sarah White, my Grandmother, L.A.H.' (Lydia Ann Hurst, 1858), and in the same hand as the first inscription: 'Worked by Sarah, wife of Thos White 1743'.

The quilt, measuring 87¼″ wide x 94½″ long, is embroidered in sections on moderately fine cream linen which is also used to back it. The embroideries have been worked in polychrome coarse silks over inked designs. The centre of the quilt has four pairs of pink carnation flowers and a bud. Their stems come to a central point, where there is another pink flower, possibly a wild rose. The embroidered leaves in pairs on either side of the stems sweep out in curves curling inwards, so that they in turn give the impression of a flower with a middle rose-like flower as its centre. Alternating between the carnation sprays Sarah has embroidered dainty little vases with twiggy branches bearing a blue pomegranate flower, some bluebells and, in pink, two other flowers. This motif is encircled with a parade of the pink carnations and stylised tulips in blue and pink interspersed with leaves. The stitches Sarah has used right throughout the quilt are satin, running, stem, cross, knot and herringbone. A diamond shape is created by then embroidering a scattering of small sprays of flowers, mainly the carnations, tulips and roses, and a pair of the tiny vases of flowers, all in pinks and blues.

An oblong is then created by placing in each corner larger sprays of the carnations and one of the tiny vases of flowers and an arc of carnations and tulips. The rest of the quilt is covered with rows of sprays of flowers and leaves scattered across it; each row is separated with dainty little twigs covered with small pink blossoms, the twigs curving downwards giving the motifs the appearance of larger-than-life floral commas. Scattered amongst the floral sprays are several delightful little embroideries each depicting a single exotic bird perched within a flowery bower.

The large central wreath is quilted with pairs of concentric rings on either side of the encircling ring of carnations and tulips. The remainder is quilted using the overlapping circle pattern known as Wineglass, which also gives the impression of a four-petalled flower. The outer edge is quilted with a row of leaves with a slightly smaller leaf within, which at first glance looks like the traditional cable motif used in quilted borders except that the ovals do not overlap each other. It is not possible to tell what has been used for batting, but since the quilt was made in England it is probably a thin layer of wool.

Although this quilt has some discoloration from the manner in which it has been folded and stored, as well as unevenness in colour from the use of different linens in the background fabric, this does not detract from its overall appearance: it remains a very attractive and elegant quilt.

Medallion Quilts

Whakatane District Museum and Gallery Quilt

This handsome old English medallion quilt, which was donated to the Whakatane Museum by Mr John Vickery, was made circa 1870. Entirely handmade, it measures 78½″ x 86½″. Although badly stained and suffering from wear, it still reveals a good use of a multitude of cottons in prints, stripes and plaids in the borders surrounding the central medallion, which features a large eight-point star of Turkey red. The borders surrounding the star are well balanced, being pieced from squares on point, triangles, long strips of fabric with squares at the corners, and a border near the edge made from half-square triangles. Holes in the surface fabric show that the batting is made of woven wool, possibly a blanket. Several patterns have been used in the quilting — chevron, clamshell, cross-hatching, floral, spirals and fleur-de-lis.

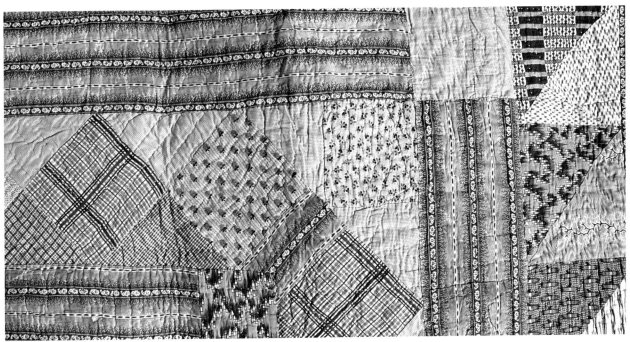

Detail of fabrics and pieced borders used to create the star medallion quilt at Whakatane District Museum and Gallery.

Medallion quilt made circa 1870 with a central star of Turkey red cotton. A wide variety of traditional quilting patterns has been used and a great number of cotton fabrics make up the borders. 78½″ x 86½″

Euphemia Ballingall Maxwell (1830–1918)

This intricately appliquéd and pieced medallion is another example of the needlework skills of Euphemia Maxwell, whose elaborate crazy quilt is shown on page (117). Family records indicate that it was made, or completed, after her arrival in New Zealand in 1865, and its layout is very typical of a classic English medallion patchwork quilt. The appliqué coverlets she made after this one were not so intricate and often featured leaves gathered from the many trees and gardens around The Elms, the mission house she inherited from her sister.

The whole coverlet measures 102″ x 102¾″ and has a central 27″ square pieced in two parts from cream cotton damask. The damask is self-patterned with woven fern fronds, and a scattering of bunches of red acorns with black and brown cups and fawn leaves. Appliquéd in the centre of the square is an English pieced eight-pointed star made from a variety of glazed chintzes patterned with small scattered flowers. The star is edged with a fine plaited black and white braid. Surrounding the large star are six smaller eight-pointed stars cut in one piece from a green and white glazed chintz and also edged with the braid. The corners of the square have appliquéd stylised tulips of Turkey red cotton, and a pair of unstemmed tulip flowers, slightly smaller, are appliquéd either side of the large star. All the tulips are edged with the braid. The tulips and other appliqué motifs overlap onto the first of five borders. Each of the five borders is different but may repeat in another size some of the motifs employed elsewhere. Striped shirting and Turkey red cotton have been used for some borders and appliqués, but it is the wide variety and beauty of the many chintzes that really delight the eye. There are charming broderie perse appliqués and many interesting design motifs. One has two bow-tie shapes superimposed over each other to form a cross and another appears to be pairs of fleur-de-lis placed end to end. There are pairs of diamonds pieced together in a chevron shape, quatrefoil shapes, and free-form flowers with eight petals. Some of the many stars have curved edges like the familiar Dresden Plate pattern. Some eight-pointed stars are small and are placed in pairs one above the other. Several fabrics are cleverly pieced, without spoiling the pattern, to make them large enough to cut the required shapes. In one area it is obvious Euphemia ran out of her favourite braid and has ended the edging abruptly, or has substituted a red channel braid.

The eight-pointed one-piece stars in the central square are amazing in their accuracy but the real *tour de force* must be the many ten- and twelve-pointed stars, each cut in one piece. These demonstrate not only that Euphemia was a skilled needlewoman, but also that she had a good knowledge of mathematics to be able to cut the stars with such precision. Her sense of design is also evidenced in the way she strategically placed her broderie perse sprays of flowers and

This spectacular appliqué quilt and the insets demonstrate the amazing design and needle skills of Euphemia Maxwell.
102" x 102¾"

curved-edged motifs to soften areas which might otherwise have been visually marred if they had had too many of the more geometric straight-edged motifs. One would go a long way before finding such a dazzling example of a traditional English medallion quilt.

Anne Romsey

Miss Eileen Frost, an old identity of Epsom, Auckland, who celebrated her 100th birthday in 1998, inherited from her mother this interesting large old patchwork coverlet. Created by Anne Romsey, an aunt of Miss Frost's maternal grandmother, it was made, or started, in 1795, according to a notation on the lining. However, noted on the reverse there is another date, 1830, which could be either the finishing date or, perhaps, the year Anne died.

The Romsey family were yeoman farmers who lived at Dedham, Suffolk, being near neighbours of the famous painter Gainsborough. Eileen's family line descent is Romsey, Keeble, Courtnall, Frost. Her father, George Frost, who numbered the author Charles Dickens amongst his friends, was a Methodist minister. He married Dora Courtnall of Sudbury, Suffolk, and his church calling took him to Coromandel, New Zealand, where Eileen was born. After Dora died in 1902, George returned to Suffolk so that his parents could take over the rearing of his little three-year-old daughter. He later remarried and the family returned to New Zealand, where his calling took him to live in many parts of the country before they finally settled in Epsom. Eileen Frost began her teaching career in 1920 after graduating from Christchurch Teachers Training College. She taught at schools all over New Zealand, presumably moving each time her family did; she was teaching at Onehunga during the 1930s Depression years, by which time the family were living in Epsom.

The coverlet, measuring 96″by 92″, is made from cotton, chintz and calico and metal templates were used to form the 3/4″ hexagons and pentagons. The white calico central portion, 27½″ by 28¼″, has appliqués cut from a palampore depicting an exotic tree with two oriental pheasants sitting on the ground below. The birds are resting on a mound of flowers; several of the flowers could be from the palampore, but other flowers, and some oak leaves with acorns, may have come from a separate piece of chintz. The sprays of flowers and leaves in the corners of the panel may also have come from two sources of fabric. The panel has a 4″ band of white calico edged each side with a lovely pale blue and brown border print.

Between these two borders, multicoloured pentagon flowers zigzag around the border, with a calico diamond appearing between the petals where the flowers join each other. In my many years of researching old quilts for this project, this is the only instance found where pentagons have been used. Most patchworkers know of several bad-luck symbols associated with the names or shapes of certain designs, and some needlewomen are known not to wish to use the pentagon. It is believed, in some folk history, to have an association with black magic, devils and witches — which is a shame, as it does make an attractive border. Anne must have thought so too as she used the same border pattern on the edges of the coverlet.

Medallion quilt made by Anne Romsey. Portions of a palampore are used in the broderie perse central square. The body of the quilt has single rows of hexagons between rows of hexagon flowers, all paper pieced. Framing borders use pentagons to create flowers — a shape very rarely used. 96" x 92"

Centre of Anne Romsey's quilt using pieces of a palampore for a broiderie perse picture.

Detail of hexagon and pentagon flowers in the Romsey quilt.

The remainder of the pieced area is composed entirely of hexagons in a pattern running diagonally across the quilt from the bottom left-hand corner to the top right-hand corner. Hexagons of white calico form the background for alternating rows of multicoloured cotton and chintz hexagon flowers and a single line of coloured hexagons, all appearing to float over the white background. The variety of prints used to create these flowers is really astonishing.

When used on her parents' large bed, the coverlet spread over the bed and draped across the floor on either side. This suggests that it could have originally been made for one of the high four-posted tester beds that sometimes necessitated the use of a set of steps to get into bed. The height of the bed from the floor allowed for the daytime stowing of a child's or maid's truckle bed. Eileen remembers that the children of the family were always warned not to step on the bedspread — which must have been difficult, for a favourite

pastime was to see if they could find any two flowers the same. Miss Frost must have continued this quest, for even up until her sight began to fail she was not able to locate two identical flowers. After the demise of her parents, the coverlet was hung from a picture-rail in the drawing room, well away from the windows, but the decades it hung there and the dust it accumulated have taken their toll on the fabrics, and the colours have faded somewhat.

Miss Frost had in her keeping the extremely fine needles used in making the patchwork and also the small metal templates. Unfortunately, at age 95, after she lost her sight completely, she had a fall and it was decided that it was time for her to transfer to a rest-home. Her friends undertook to clear her house for her. Sadly, they did not know about the templates and needles, which should have gone with the coverlet when it was donated to the Auckland War Memorial Museum quilt collection, so these have disappeared forever.

The McClure Quilt

Miss M. D. Connor, who lived in the next street to Miss Eileen Frost and was also a schoolteacher, inherited a very attractive and interesting quilt from her mother, whose maiden name was McClure. The McClures were of Huguenot descent and lived in County Antrim, Ireland, where the quilt was made circa 1870. Miss Connor's mother brought it to New Zealand in 1911. It is not known if she actually made the quilt or whether it was made by another member of the family.

Quilt made circa 1870 belonging to Miss S. H. McClure, County Antrim, Ireland. A medallion quilt with the central panel especially manufactured for use in quilts, it is pieced in the appliquéd borders, with cross stitch used to attach the appliqués. 103″ x 106″

Detail of the printed panel in Miss McClure's quilt.

This medallion quilt measures 103″ x 106″ and has at its centre one of the spectacular glazed chintz panels especially manufactured for making medallion quilts. Printed on white, it pictures a beautiful bouquet of mixed flowers surrounded by a floral wreath, and in each corner of the square is a large flower with sprays of smaller flowers coming from either side at right angles to the main flower. The square is framed with a 1½″ wide border of a floral chintz which has a light greyish-beige background. This is followed by a 3″ wide white cotton border with spaced appliqués of alternate flowers and leaves which appear to have been cut from the same chintz as the first (1½″ wide) and the next, 3¼″ wide, border. The next border after that, which is 5″ wide,

is pieced from 3¼″ floral chintz squares on point and white cotton triangles, and is then followed by another 3¼″ border, of the same chintz as the previous borders. Then comes a 6″ white border with larger chintz flower appliqués. A different floral chintz with a tan background is introduced for the next border, which is 5¼″ wide, followed by another border, 6¼″, of 5″ chintz squares on point with white cotton triangles. The gradual widening of each border gives a pleasing balance to the whole top, which is then completed with two different fabrics, one being used top and bottom and the other for either side. However, these fabrics are not of the same quality or general tonings as the rest of the quilt and have possibly been added at a later stage in the quilt's life.

The central square and the outer borders have been quilted with a chevron pattern and all other seams right throughout are quilted ¼″ either side. The appliqué motifs are stitched in place with fine cross-stitching and have a line of quilting close to their edges on the background cotton, and although the quilt is cotton lined there is no batting.

This quilt, also, is now in the care of the Auckland War Memorial Museum.

Crazy Quilts

A popular type of quilt that used embroidery as an embellishment was the elaborate crazy quilt much beloved by Victorian needlewomen. Not only did they use as many lavish and interesting fabrics as they could collect, but they also demonstrated all the wonderful and interesting embroidery stitches in their repertoire, to cover the linking seams and to stitch the little pictures they often over-embroidered onto the odd-shaped scraps. Besides embroidery silks, gold and silver metallic threads, sequins and beads would often also add to the needlework *tour de force* these crazy quilts became.

Euphemia Ballingall Maxwell (1830–1918)

Euphemia Ballingall Johnston was born in the year 1830 to Barbara Dougal Johnston and her husband Alexander Johnston of Aberdeen, Scotland. As Euphemia was raised, like many good Scots, within the Presbyterian religion, it was not surprising that she should marry a Presbyterian minister — the Reverend Andrew Maxwell. As soon as Andrew was ordained into the ministry in 1853, the young couple sailed for Australia, where upon arrival they travelled to Armidale in northern New South Wales. After several years of service at Armidale, Andrew was transferred to Kilmore, just north of Melbourne in the State of Victoria, where the couple and their growing brood of children lived until Andrew's untimely death in 1865. During her marriage to Andrew, Euphemia was delivered of seven children. Though her first-born, Euphemia, and two sons died as infants, the other four — Andrew, Edith Duff, Alice Heron and Ebenezer — were fine, healthy children.

Following her husband's death, Euphemia and her children, after having packed up all their furniture and other belongings, sailed to Wellington, New Zealand where they took refuge with her brother Judge Johnston. Six months later she purchased a small place in Wadestown, which in those days was in the bush. The moving of her possessions to the new home was no easy task, for amongst her furniture was a piano, and the route was rough, muddy and in parts steep. (The house Euphemia bought is still at

Euphemia Maxwell's crazy patchwork quilt is one of the finest examples of Victorian needlework in New Zealand. 71" x 92"

Euphemia Maxwell

Wadestown as it has an historic building preservation classification.)

Mrs Maxwell's sister Christina (née Johnston) was the second wife of the missionary Archdeacon Alfred Nesbit Brown and lived at the mission house called The Elms at Tauranga. When the Reverend Brown died in 1883 he left The Elms to his wife, and when Christina passed away in 1887 she bequeathed the property to Euphemia, who once again packed up her worldly goods, including the piano, and moved to Tauranga, where she spent the rest of her life.

Euphemia was a very artistic and accomplished needlewoman. Amongst examples of her handwork are some splatter-work curtains. This technique consists of placing cut-out shapes in a pleasing pattern on the fabric and then flipping paint over the uncovered surface in a splattering of small spots so that when the shaped pieces are lifted the whole effect is of a reverse transfer. Euphemia used leaves from the garden for her templates. It is easy to visualise her strolling about the garden paths selecting interesting leaves from which to develop patterns.

Euphemia made two interesting large appliquéd medallion-style coverlets (pages 109–110), one of which includes leaf shapes along with the other more traditional designs. The second of the two medallion coverlets is a delightful melange of broderie perse and other appliqué as well as some English pieced stars also appliquéd in place. The fabric used is mainly glazed chintz and some motifs have an added embellishment of fine braiding. The two appliqué coverlets, when sent to England for exhibition along with other work of 'ladies from the Colonies', won prizes, the certificates for which are still at The Elms. The coverlets, together with Euphemia's magnificent crazy patchwork quilt, were also exhibited in Wellington at the New Zealand Centenary Exhibition in 1940.

The crazy patchwork quilt must be one of the finest examples of this type of Victorian needlework in New Zealand. It measures 71″ x 92″ and the materials used are all luxurious silks, velvets, brocades and ribbons in stripes, prints, plaids, checks and plain unpatterned fabric. Every colour in the spectrum is present and each seam line is covered with one of a wide variety of fancy embroidered stitches. Nearly every individual piece has something embroidered on it — a fantastic variety of subjects, such as animals (elephant, deer, a pig and a rat), birds, insects (a scarab, butterflies and a spider's web), and a cobra that rears its head. There are flowers and a sheaf of wheat, vases and urns; there are faces, a moon and stars, and hearts. There is a shoe, scissors, a sword hilt and a dagger, a tennis net, and close by a tennis racket and ball; there is a sailing boat and a kite. Music is represented by a treble clef and some crotchets, a harp, guitar, lute and drum. There is some Greek writing, and other symbols, and one piece has Euphemia's full name embroidered on it. Many pieces are beaded, sequinned, braided, or have gold metallic threads couched in place. She must have had fun devising something new to include in this wonderful quilt, and what glee the younger family members must have had in looking for their favourite little picture.

The top is framed with a border of dark olive green velvet (6¼″ wide at top and bottom and 7″ wide on the sides) which is mitred at the corners. There is an inter-lining of cotton twill and the quilt is backed with cherry red satin.

Euphemia worked on this quilt from 1887, completing it just prior to her death in 1918, and it is an amazing specimen of a superb crazy patchwork quilt. It is to be passed on to Euphemia's great-granddaughter Christine Major Tait (Mr Duff Maxwell's daughter) who is also a quilter. Mrs Tait's daughter, Clair King, and her daughters too, are continuing the family tradition of quiltmaking, so the wonderful crazy quilt will have three more generations of quiltmakers to care for and treasure it.

Mrs Maxwell was quite a character of a lady and was often referred to locally as 'Queen Victoria', 'Lady Maxwell', or 'The Duchess', and although not a member of either the royal family or the peerage, she had no objection to the use of these titles. From photographic portraits (opposite) of her, she certainly had the bearing of a lady of quality. She was always on the lookout for wonderful fabrics for making her crazy patchwork quilt, and visiting gentlemen were advised to keep out of arm's reach if they were wearing a handsome necktie — it was not unknown for Euphemia to produce her scissors and snip off a piece!

Neither of Euphemia's daughters married and because her eldest grandson Grant was in failing health and there was the prospect of two lots of death duties having to be paid out on the estate, the property of The Elms was bequeathed to her younger grandson, Duff Maxwell, the son of Euphemia's son Ebenezer. The Elms mission house and grounds remain the property of the Maxwell family and there is a wealth of records, furniture and effects stored within the house, library, chapel and Fencible cottage. A trust has been set up to maintain the property and catalogue the accumulation of family documents and possessions, which form a veritable treasure trove of early New Zealand history.

The Morris Crazy Quilt

Nothing is known about the place or date of birth, or parents, of Mrs Morris, except that she was English. From her first marriage she had a son, Edward Parnell, who was born on 16 December 1815 and died on 19 May 1883 aged 68. She later married a Mr Morris. One could speculate that one or both of her husbands were of comfortable means, as Edward must have entered the Royal Navy as a cadet officer: he became a Commander at age 34. He must have left the navy then, though: in December 1849 he was known to be trading in the *Mary Jones* at Smyrna (now known as Izmir). This city, at the head of the Gulf of Smyrna, was the chief commercial trading centre for the Levant, especially for figs, raisins, tobacco and carpets. During periods when England was not at war it was common for army and naval personnel to leave the services, but they could be called back at the King's command should the country find itself at war again.

The crazy quilt was made by Mrs Morris as a gift to her son — it is believed, on the occasion of his marriage. Though it is in a fragile state now it still retains a lot of its charm. The fabrics used include cotton, brocade, taffeta, grosgrain, plush velvet, painted velvet, ribbons and paisley patterns, in a wide range of colours. There are solids, prints, stripes, plaids, checks and polka dots and a wonderful array of embroidered embellishments. These include flowers, both individual and in sprays; acorns; leaves; and fans.

Details from the Morris crazy quilt.

More masculine motifs include a dog's head, a ship's wheel, a crescent moon, stars (a navigational aid?), an axe and a fence.

The motifs that indicate it was a wedding quilt include in several places two linked rings, a good luck spiderweb, and a chimney sweep with his ladder and long-handled brush. For a long time in England it has been considered that good luck would shine on a bride if, as she left her home for the wedding ceremony, there was a chimney sweep standing at the door to give her a kiss before she entered her carriage. Also embroidered, in sweeping lettering, are the initials 'JMc'. Nobody knows if these were Mrs Morris's initials or whether they could possibly be those of the bride. The letters are embroidered in pale

Crazy patchwork made circa 1840 by Mrs Morris for her son Edward Parnell (from her first marriage) as a wedding gift. 86″ x 86 ½″

Young Commander Parnell would have been familiar with lotus flowers and waterlilies seen during his travels.

The embroidered initials are embellished with lily-of-the-valley, a favourite flower for wedding bouquets.

blue satin-stitch, embellished with metallic thread and surrounded with lily-of-the-valley sprays. The quilt has an inner lining of sturdy ticking and an outer lining of flesh-coloured sateen.

This old crazy quilt is now owned by another Mrs Morris, no relation to the original family, but a friend of one of the descendants of Commander Parnell.

Sarah Hannah Armstrong Wood (circa 1860–1930)

Sarah Hannah Armstrong was the daughter of Mr and Mrs Jefferson Armstrong, the son and daughter-in-law of Nancy Jefferson Armstrong who made the Waterloo coverlet (see page 133). Sarah was born at Park House, the family home of her father. She wed John Wood, a businessman of some substance, who built and owned many properties. At one time he owned a substantial drapery business. This business may have been the source of many of the lovely fabrics Sarah used to make the crazy patchwork quilt she stitched in 1900. She used some beautiful silk and satin floral prints, and brocades, as well as some solids and other prints. The segment joins are over-embellished with cream feather stitching.

The pieced area is 49″ by 56½″ and is completed with an 8″ wide gold sateen frill. The reverse side has a central block, 16″ by 15¾″, made up of multi-coloured plain sateens roughly 1″ square. Many of these are very bright. Some have the letter X and numbers printed on them, which may indicate that they are sample fabrics from Mr Wood's drapery shop. This block is surrounded by borders of varying widths, two in rose pink separated by one in pale turquoise green and cream, and top and bottom a pretty print of pink floral stripes and pink sprays of flowers on a cream background.

There is no batting, but the two layers are hand quilted together in a large clamshell pattern in red and gold thread. Although the bulk of the quilt has been hand-stitched the piecing on the reverse side, and the edges where the frill is attached, have been machine sewn.

Sarah and John had one son, John, who came to settle in New Zealand, and late in their lives they joined him. Sarah brought with her not only the crazy quilt but also the Waterloo quilt that her grandmother had made. These two quilts are now in the care of two of Sarah's granddaughters.

Sarah Wood's crazy patchwork quilt plus frilled edge, probably made circa 1880–90 using sample fabrics from her husband's drapery business. 94″ x 56½″

Turkey Red Quilts

For many centuries, cotton fabric dyed red posed a problem for European textile manufacturers. They could provide brilliantly fast-dyed red silk and woollen fabrics but could not overcome the difficulties they encountered with cotton, which had a resistance to the dyeing processes they used. A fabric would start as a bright red but would fade and change. This unreliability meant that red was rarely used in quiltmaking, because no quiltmaker would wish her masterwork to be marred by either a red patch bleeding dye or a once-bright red soon fading into an entirely different shade.

The area of the Mediterranean east of Greece, known as the Levant, had always produced great dyed yarns and fabrics, especially in wonderful blues and reds. The reliability of these coloured yarns manifested itself particularly well in the beautiful designs of the carpet makers. Many of the dye-works were centred in Turkey, especially in the northern part in the vicinity of Adrianople. The dye technique used by the Turks to produce their much-sought-after red yarn entailed in excess of a dozen stages spaced out over several months, which of course had a bearing on the price they could demand for the finished product. This technique was an intricate and well-kept trade secret until the eighteenth century, when industrial espionage, much feared in the dye trade for centuries, eventually succeeded. Before long, both English and French textile mills had another item to add to the catalogue of fabrics they could provide — reliable and famous Turkey red cottons!

The period from about 1830 to the turn of the century saw a proliferation of Turkey red and white quilts. The reliability of the red cotton was well proved, and because vast amounts of the fabric were being manufactured the price became well within the means of many quilters. A whole new breed of quilts blossomed. It was such a dramatic colour to use with white, and many adventurous women took up the challenge to create a red and white quilt. Away went the small pieces of cotton and intricate patterns, and along came large bold geometric designs. The large plain areas provided ample space for the quilter to demonstrate her stitching ability by using a wonderful array of traditional quilting patterns hitherto mainly used in whole-cloth quilts. Other, not so daring, women began to use their Turkey red fabrics skilfully scattered about to enhance their more traditionally pieced designs, and the colour was also a valued addition to the appliqué experts' palettes.

Elizabeth Carson (née Boyd, circa 1850s)

Elizabeth Carson made this spectacular Turkey red and white quilt in the mid-nineteenth century, soon after the reliable red fabric became available.

Mrs Kath Webster of Auckland is the owner of this handsome Turkey red quilt. It was made by her great-grandmother Elizabeth Carson (née Boyd). She was born at Whiteside's Corner, near Ballymena, Northern Ireland (date unknown, probably mid-nineteenth century) and her shopkeeper husband's general store is still in Ballymena. Elizabeth had three sons and a daughter. In 1908, after she became a widow, she, her youngest son and her daughter joined the two eldest sons who had already settled in New Zealand. A skilled needlewoman, Elizabeth Carson doubtless made many quilts, judging by the quality of the quilting in the Turkey red quilt which she brought with her from Ireland. Another of her quilts was inherited by Mrs Webster's sister and is a Puss in the Corner and Nine Patch variation. Mrs Carson was also known to have done tapestry work.

Whakatane District Museum and Gallery Quilts

The Whakatane District Museum and Gallery has two fine examples of Turkey red and white quilts. One, donated by Mr G. Forbes of Opotiki, was made by Sarah Pridhoe North some years before she left England to come to New Zealand in 1870. Its striking red cross and red and white concentric borders are closely and beautifully quilted with flowers, fans, cables, trellis grids, scallops and conch shells.

The second, a coverlet donated by Mrs Francis of Whakatane, was made in Rarotonga. It consists of a large white cotton sheet appliquéd similarly to Hawaiian quilts, with four large American eagles, each with a shield and holding arrows in one talon and a spray of leaves — probably an olive branch — in the other, surrounding a large eight-point star in an ornate circle. There are other leafy branches around the edge. The entire red area has been cut in one piece. There is no lining or quilting.

Top: The red and white quilt made by Sarah Pridhoe North, 84" x 99". The photograph above shows her fine quilting, the fan pattern being one of the many traditional quilting patterns she has stitched into this quilt.

The appliquéd coverlet from Mrs Francis is 102" x 107" in size and was made in Rarotonga. This photograph shows the central portion, which has been designed using the folding technique perfected by the Hawaiians.

The Dykes Quilt

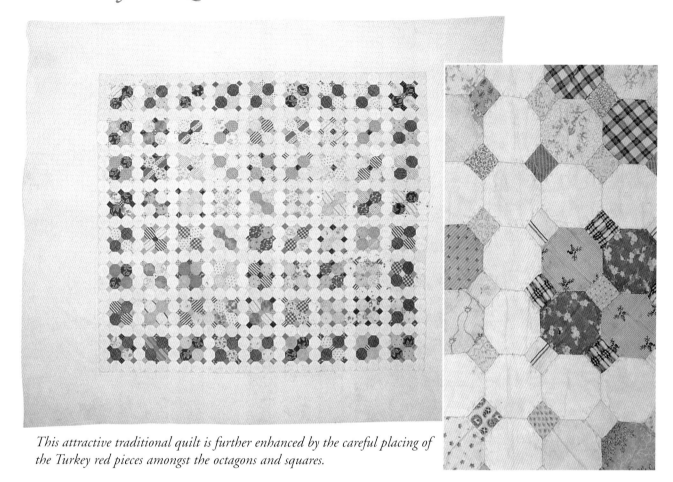

This attractive traditional quilt is further enhanced by the careful placing of the Turkey red pieces amongst the octagons and squares.

Mrs M. McCurdy of Hamilton is the proud owner of this quilt, which she inherited from her mother, Edith Jean Paton (née Dykes), who was born on 25 May 1899 at Tynemouth, England, the eldest of her mother's children. Edith's early years were not very happy as her mother, Margaret Augusta Dykes (née Davidson), died when Edith was nine years old. Being the eldest child, Edith was expected to forgo her schooling and stay home to do the housekeeping and look after her siblings and father. However, her father remarried, and at the age of thirteen she was sent out to work in a restaurant.

Edith was probably a good churchgoing young woman for when she was 21 a kind Baptist family arranged for her to emigrate with them to New Zealand. Amongst the items the young Edith brought with her was a much-treasured quilt, which had belonged to her mother, Margaret.

The quilt is believed to have been made by either Margaret or her mother. It has been skilfully made, and judging by the fabrics used, and depending upon which of these two women made the quilt, it could have been made prior to the 1850s. It is well designed and a good example of the use of Turkey red, both in the octagons in the outer blocks and in the strategically placed small squares scattered amongst the other blocks, which gives the whole top a pleasing balance of design.

The Ecclesfield Quilt

At the West Coast Historical Museum in Hokitika there is a patchwork bedspread which was donated by the Ecclesfield family of Kowhaitirangi, early settlers in Hokitika. In the mid-1860s this family were merchants there; the rates roll of the Hokitika Borough Council records Esther Ecclesfield in 1867 as owning a property at the north end of Revell Street comprising five sections of land. In 1871 the merchants were again listed, but by 1898 the firm must have closed down their business as only Mrs Ecclesfield is listed, as living in a cottage and paying rates on a property at Stafford Street.

The bedspread is Turkey red and white in a traditional Windmill pattern. Each triangle in the pattern has been cross-stitched in a wide range of non-repeating designs, red stitching on the white segments and white on the red, each pair of triangles forming 7″ squares. The pieced and embroidered area is surrounded by a 10½″ red border which includes, towards the outer edge, a 3″ floral cross-stitched border. Towards one side of the quilt are three red triangles, each with a different embroidered inscription. One has the initials E.E.E. with HOKA on the line below, another has SEPT with 1888 below and the third has MW with CHCH below. The triple E initials could very well belong to Esther Ecclesfield. The cover is lined but there is no batting or quilting. The quilt measures 77″ x 99″.

The Ecclesfield quilt is another spectacular use of Turkey red and white. 77″ x 99″

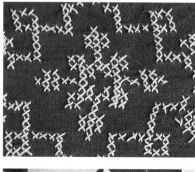

Details of the red and white cross stitch embroidery used in the 176 triangles and the outer border.

Museum of Transport and Technology Quilt

Detail from Grandmother's Garden quilt made by Martha Gordon Carrie. See pages 130–131 for image of entire quilt.

Auckland's Museum of Transport and Technology (MOTAT) has in its quilt collection a pair of Turkey red and white quilts. One is made in a sort of Robbing Peter to Pay Paul method. The other is a handsome finely-quilted American Cherry Basket quilt which has the added interest of having two of the baskets lying on their sides — the kind of deliberate mistake we quilters often call 'God's patch'. As only God can make something perfect, some quilting groups include a deliberate mistake so that they are not seen to be trying to outdo God.

Another in the collection is an attractive hexagon Grandmother's Flower Garden quilt which uses the red for the centre of each flower and for the wide bordering frame. Martha Gordon, who was born in Carnouslie, Scotland, commenced to make the flowers in the 1860s before coming to New Zealand. She travelled on the *Ganges,* arriving in Auckland on 12 October 1863. The quilt was completed after her arrival in New Zealand and she probably pieced some of the hexagon flowers on the long journey out. The quilt would have been a bright and pretty part of the dowry she brought with her when, in 1865, she married Isaac Carrie in the home of Mr James Miller in Newton, Auckland.

Grandmother's Garden quilt made by Martha Gordon Carrie between 1863–65. It uses 2" hexagons to make up the flowers. The pieced patchwork has then been appliquéd to a wide border of Turkey red cotton. The lining is in three pieces with Turkey red cotton stitched on either side of a wide piece of Paisley printed cotton. The lining fabrics are machine stitched together and the corners have been mitred using a sewing machine. 91 1/2" x 98"

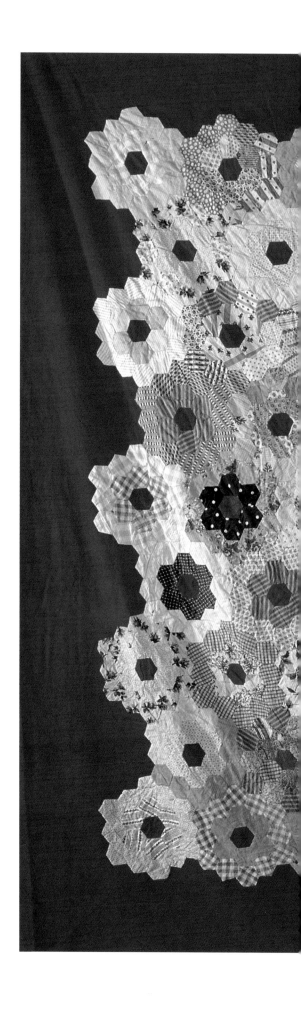

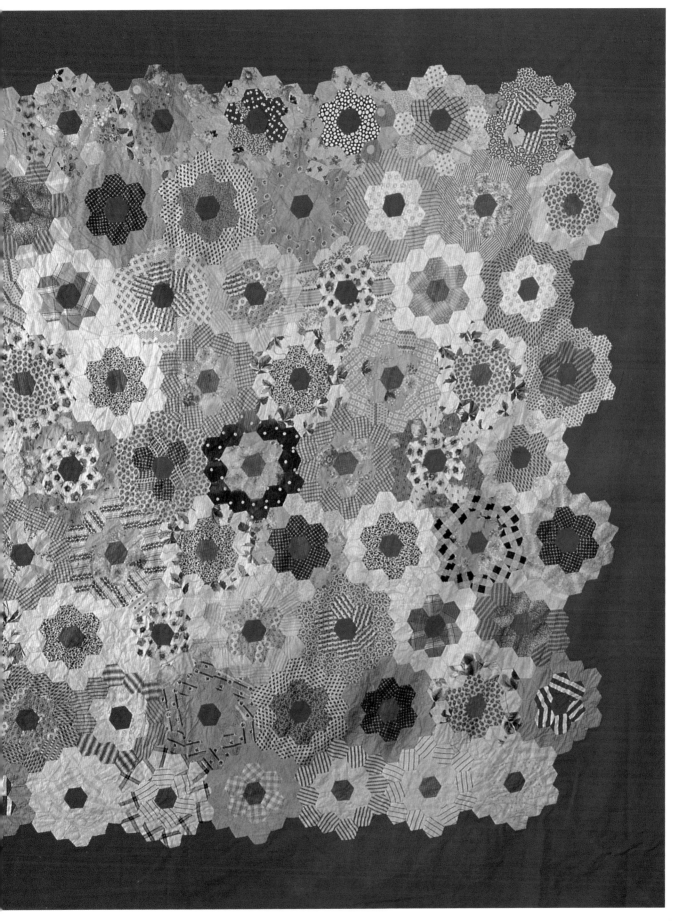

Wartime Quilts

Down through the centuries there has always been a link between wars and quilts. The banners and flags of knights of old were pieced together using patchwork techniques, and legend has it that the returning Crusaders introduced quilting to England after seeing the bodily protection from sword slashes provided to the Saracens by the wearing of quilted vests. Many Asian countries used quilted clothing not only for warmth but also for protection in battle situations, and Japanese firefighters also wore quilted garments to protect their bodies from flames.

In the United States during both the War of Independence and the Civil War, maps, secret documents and even medicines were sometimes moved through enemy territories hidden within layers of quilts. As well as silverware and other treasures, quilts went into hiding (often underground) to save them from marauding plunderers. Freedom quilts, given to young men when they left home, often went off to war with young recruits to be used as their bedrolls, and sadly often became their shrouds. It was not unusual for quilts to be retrieved from battlefields off the backs of dead horses or mules.

The North Carolina Quilt Project documented one beautiful medallion quilt that survived the Civil War. When a North Carolina doctor went out onto a battlefield to attend the wounded and dying, he saw this quilt on the back of a dead mule, having been used as a saddle blanket. Recognising the quilt as typical of those from the southern States, he rescued it and sent it home to his mother for cleaning and mending, and from then onwards it has been used for special guests only in the homes of his descendants. This quilt may have been a dead soldier's own quilt, or could have been part of his 'spoils of war'.

There is a family in Northland who cherish a patchwork coverlet which was pieced by one of their foremothers while she was waiting for her husband to return from the Battle of Waterloo (opposite). The Philips family quilt (on page 93) also has a tenuous thread linking it to the Napoleonic Wars: the maker's father, fearing for the safety of his wife and two young daughters when it looked very probable that Napoleon and his hot-blooded French soldiers were about to invade England, shipped the three of them off to America to family connections in Boston.

Some convalescing soldiers from the Napoleonic wars were known to have made quilts as part of their occupational therapy and to help while away the long hours waiting for their injured bodies to mend.

Nancy Jefferson Armstrong (circa 1780s)

Nancy Jefferson is believed to have been born in 1780 at Bowness in the county of Cumberland, England. She married into the Armstrong family of Park House, Silloth, also in the county of Cumberland. Though she had many siblings, she and

her husband had only one son, Jefferson, in 1820.

The Jeffersons were farmers and quite famous for breeding fine shire horses. However, Nancy's husband was a trained navigator, and in 1815 he was serving with the Yeomen of the Guards at the Battle of

The medallion style with a 'Chips and Whetstone' pattern in a circle in the centre of Nancy Armstrong's Waterloo quilt.

Waterloo. Doubtless to occupy some of the lonely hours whilst she awaited the return of her husband from this famous battle, Nancy made a very handsome cotton patchwork bedcover. It measures 8′4″ by 8′11″ and is pieced in a medallion style.

The central square is dominated by a very well-constructed 'Chips and Whetstone' block, surrounded by four individual stars at the centre of each side, and has a hexagon flower in each corner. The four borders that surround the central block gradually increase in width and all have a different set of block designs at the corners. Two of these borders are pieced squares on point, and the remaining two have a variety of blocks appliquéd at measured spaces. These consist of hexagon flowers, eight-point stars, divided circles, and an interesting block of pairs of two colours of a teardrop shape. This is a German folk design called *fylfot*, thought to represent good and evil. There is a

fabulous array of small prints used in this top; they have been well placed to complement each other, and several have been pieced to provide sufficient fabric to complete a segment. The top is lined with a cream cotton; it has no binding but is finished with the edges turned in edge to edge. There is no batting or quilting. The colours show no signs of fading, and apart from slight age staining it is hard to believe that this coverlet is in such good shape after all these years.

After his return from the Battle of Waterloo Nancy's husband was employed to teach navigation at Greenrow Academy, a Quaker educational establishment at Silloth. The Waterloo quilt came to New Zealand with Nancy's granddaughter Sarah Wood (page 122) when she and her husband late in life joined their only son, John, who had earlier emigrated to this country. The quilt is now in the care of one of Nancy's great-great-granddaughters.

Crimea Quilt

The Auckland War Memorial Museum has in its collection of quilts one which was made by a veteran of the Crimean War, 1854–56, possibly as part of his occupational therapy. How this quilt (opposite) came to New Zealand is not known. The soldier would not have been a member of the Fencibles who were

brought to the Auckland area to set up a ring of settlements to defend the growing town, as the last of these villages was established in 1852. One possibility is that, if the Crimean War veteran was still a regular in the Imperial Army when the New Zealand Wars broke out in the 1860s, he could have come to this country

Crimean War quilt from the collection of Auckland War Memorial Museum. 94" x 96⁷/₈".

as part of the army reinforcements, and subsequently decided to take his discharge here. Who knows?

The Sarjeant Gallery at Wanganui has a collection of Te Kooti memorabilia which includes a personal flag pieced together in the manner of patchwork, and a fragment of an English patchwork quilt, believed to have been taken from one of the early settler homes he raided. The story goes that he was using up the quilt piece by piece to clean the barrel of his gun, which is also part of the collection.

During World War II the wife of General Freyberg assembled a group of women who, though not strictly members of the armed services, were directly under army command and were thus provided with army paybooks and transport. These women were called Tuis and they set up branches of the Fernleaf Club in cities where New Zealand armed servicemen would take their leave, such as Cairo, London and various Italian cities. It was reported that these women had made a quilt, but this information was soon denied by surviving members. However, one ex-Tui solved the mystery by suggesting that it was the Spinsters' Club of Wellington who were the quiltmakers.

An ex-Army nurse (also a quilter) told of her leave trips to London when she would stay at the Fernleaf Club. This club was situated in a house in a row of several dwellings (now demolished) in Lowndes Square, Knightsbridge, which were used for leave accommodation for several groups of the armed forces

from abroad — including New Zealand, Canada and Poland. Because the glass from the windows in the houses had been blown out by the blitz attacks, the bedrooms were so cold that the guests would often sleep in their uniforms and greatcoats. After the Americans came into the war the drop-in centres that the American Red Cross established were supplied with crates of wonderful, warm patchwork quilts.

American quilters produced thousands of quilts to be sent to England and Europe to help keep refugees, bombed-out householders and service people warm in this time of great destruction. The news of the presence of these quilts soon filtered through to Barbara Freyberg, who, as the wife of a famous resourceful army general versed in foraging techniques, also knew there were always ways and means of acquiring the necessities of life for her troops. It transpired that the Tuis received regular supplies of large tins of golden New Zealand butter, a commodity of great rarity in war-torn England, so the astute lady proceeded to barter her 'New Zealand gold' for American patchwork quilts. From then onwards, the fortunate Kiwi servicemen and women who took their leave breaks in London and could find a bed in the Fernleaf Club had the comfort of much-appreciated warm quilts.

Signature Quilts

At the outbreak of World War II a group of young Wellington ladies who used to meet regularly for lunch thought it would be a great idea to volunteer as drivers for the army officers — that is, until they found this would necessitate their joining the WACCs and learning the intricacies of vehicle maintenance, etc. — not at all what they had in mind. Mrs Patience Hyams, the mother of Miss Peg Hyams, one of the group of young ladies, suggested they do as she and her friends had done during World War I and form themselves into the Spinsters' Club, which is what they did. They would meet trains bringing young service personnel on leave and invite them to their meeting place. There they would provide refreshments and somewhere to relax in a homely atmosphere; perhaps sew a newly acquired chevron onto a tunic sleeve; help some to

Detail of a World War II signature quilt made by Red Cross Durie Hill Sun Centre and The Wanganui Women's Club.

write letters home; and arrange socials and perhaps a dance or two.

To raise money for the patriotic fund they decided to further follow in the footsteps of the first Spinsters' Club and make a signature quilt. They were each provided with squares of fabric and would visit, or waylay, as many people as they could and request that they give a donation and sign their names on the square of material. It became quite a competition to get really important folk to contribute cash and signatures. Once the square was filled with names the signatures would be embroidered. When sufficient embroidered squares had been collected, they were stitched together in an attractive manner to form a 'quilt' top. After the lining had been added the edges would be neatly bound. Thus they were not actually quilts, but rather coverlets, as they were not batted and neither quilted nor tied.

More funds could be raised by putting the completed item on display. In many parts of the world signature quilts have frequently been made as fundraisers; they have also been made as a farewell memory gift, to a friend, or maybe to a popular clergyman or teacher who was leaving the district.

Because Wellington is the seat of government and many companies had their head offices in the capital, the two Spinsters' Club quilts abound with the signatures of politicians of the time, and important businessmen. One signature that almost leaps off the

E.H. Shackleton's signature can be seen near the stain on this World War I Spinsters' Club signature quilt.

1916–17 quilt top is that of E.H. Shackleton, the famous Antarctic explorer. Other signatures that stand out on this quilt are W.J. and R.A. Massey, F.O.V. Acheson, Wm. Waddel, E.D. Bell, J.G. and Theresa Ward, Maui Pomare, and Myers. Some of the signatures noted on the 1939–40 Spinsters' Club quilt are those of Scots-born tenor Heddle Nash and English soprano Isobel Baillie — famous and very popular operatic duetists who were on a concert tour of New Zealand timed to coincide with the 1940 Centennial celebrations and Exhibition being held in Wellington. Two of the political signatures are K. Holyoake and A. O'Shea, but well-known names are too numerous to list them all.

Miss Hyams donated both of the Spinsters' Club quilts to the Queen Elizabeth II Army Museum at Waiouru, and further investigation revealed that the museum in fact has a collection of seven of these interesting quilts. Two were made in 1916 in the Invercargill / Bluff area and another at Southland Technical College. They are quite delightful as, besides signatures, many embroidered patriotic pictures and slogans are scattered about the surfaces. Another World War II top is a sheet with signatures embroidered in red and blue. It appears to have been made by people, possibly wives or fiancées with connections to various regiments, as R.A.C. Buffs Hawke's Bay and 1st A.I.F. appear amongst the names. The seventh quilt was made during World War II by

members of the Red Cross Durie Hill Sub Centre and the Wanganui Women's Club. Besides having a handsomely pieced version of the New Zealand flag on the reverse and signatures on the front, the front corners bear the names of such heroes as J.A. Ward V.C., W.D. Brown D.F.C., S.I. Millen D.F.C. and A.C. Deere D.F.C. The last-mentioned of these acquired more decorations as the war progressed and was also the leader of the famous Dam Busters.

A newspaper cutting sent to the author reports the story of another 1918 signature quilt (sometimes referred to as an embroidered tablecloth) with over 1,000 embroidered signatures collected by the Patriotic Society around the Malvern area of the South Island. This was known as the Great Quilt and emerged again as a fundraiser during World War II, when for a donation of 10 shillings people were challenged to guess the number of signatures. There would doubtless have been some enthusiasm engendered among the locals to see if they could locate a signature of older family members and friends. Unfortunately no address was provided to follow up this quilt for photographic purposes.

The female members of the Spencer family of Ngatawhakawhaka sheep station in the Tolaga Bay

World war II signature quilt made by the Red Cross Durie Hill Sub Centre and the Wanganui Women's Club.

area, whose family heirloom quilt is pictured on page 89, during World War II kept up a continuous supply of food parcels to England. They had many friends and family connections in England, as it was customary for young Englishmen to come to their sheep station as cadets to learn how to become competent farmers. Each parcel, weighing 11 lb, contained a rich fruit cake or tin of gingernut biscuits, dripping rendered down and soldered up in Glaxo or dried milk tins, and tins of meat. Using a German recipe they also processed their home-produced butter

(by a fairly long method) so that while still hot it could be run off into tins which would then be soldered closed. Butter preserved using this method would keep at least a year.

These busy women also made 100 children's dresses for evacuees sent from the cities into the comparative safety of the English countryside. They collected up the coloured fleeces, which had no value for export, and were not sought after as they are today by craft workers. They spun these fleeces and then knitted the prepared yarn into jumpers for the merchant navy crews on the Russian convoys. The fleeces were not washed before spinning so the wool retained its lanolin and was thus more or less waterproof and admirable for knitting seamen's socks and sweaters.

The poorer-grade wool and combings were washed and teased out to make them light and fluffy and then used for batting in quilts. Each quilt required six yards of fabric and many designs were used. With their soft wool batting the quilts were delightfully light and warm. At that time there was no electricity at Ngatawhakawhaka so the children's dresses and the quilts would have been made with a trusty treadle machine. Over 100 of these quilts were sewn and sent directly to Lord Bledisloe (a past Governor-General of New Zealand and acquaintance of the family), who distributed them to various military hospitals. No information was provided to reveal where the fabric was obtained during a time of austerity when ration books ruled everyone's lives. Dress fabric, clothing, household linens and furnishing fabrics were only obtainable by handing over precious clothing coupons along with the purchase price. The ladies must have canvassed far and wide to collect scraps and remnants of material to create not only the quilts (600 yards of material in all) but also the 100 children's dresses.

In February 1942, when Singapore fell to the Japanese invading army, nearly 3,000 British and allied nationals were imprisoned in the dreaded Changi Prison. Included in this number were 500 women and children. Many did not know if their husbands, relatives and friends had survived the fighting, or whether they had been imprisoned, at Changi or elsewhere in other POW camps. Nor did the women have any means of communication to let their loved ones know of their own whereabouts. At the suggestion of a member of the Red Cross, they decided to make quilts in the hope that the Japanese would allow these to be delivered to the POW camps, and thus at least some of their menfolk might find out that they were still alive.

The women who participated in this project were each given a square of white cotton and commenced to embroider pictures, emblems and signatures. Australian, Canadian, Dutch, English, New Zealand and Scottish nationalities are obviously apparent amongst the emblems and messages. Three of these quilts were made, each containing 66 blocks, and on the reverse sides were embroidered messages indicating that the quilts were made by the women prisoners of Changi Internment Camp, one for the Australian wounded soldiers, one for the British soldiers and the third for the Japanese soldiers. The messages also included a clause that upon the cessation of hostilities the quilts should go to the Red Cross of Australia and Britain. The quilts survived the war and were located at one of the POW camp hospitals. The Red Cross took the British one back to England to their training headquarters, but as the Japanese didn't show any desire to have the one made for their soldiers (possibly because of the dishonour engendered by defeat), Australian Army Medical Officer Colonel R.M. Webster took it, and the quilt made for the Australian soldiers, back to Australia. Many years later all three quilts were reunited and put into the care of the Australian War Memorial organisation. They are now housed together on display at Treloar Technology Centre in Mitchell, Australian Capital Territory.

In more recent times, quilts were made during the 'Desert Storm' war, both in the United States and by some of the servicewomen involved in the war. Also, following the destructive conflict that consumed much of the former Yugoslavia, many quilts were despatched to this war-torn area. Wars come and go and still today the therapy of the making, giving or receiving of a quilt is continuing the magic message of a special kind of loving and caring.

Bibliography

Since becoming interested in old patchwork and quilting in the early 1970s I have read copiously anything I could find on the subject in newspapers, countless magazine articles and dozens of books. As well, I have corresponded and had many discussions with like-minded women in England, the United States and Canada. To single out what to list under this heading is almost an impossible task, so I have selected and listed the books, magazines and women who have contributed most to my knowledge on this subject. Many of the owners of old New Zealand quilts have provided information from family documents. In some instances these families have shared with me small books that have been written about their pioneer families; most of these books are unavailable to the general public, and some are long out of print. I have included the titles of several books which I have used for references which, though they may not mention quilts in other than a fleeting sentence, have enabled me to trace the progression of quilting as it has resulted from a certain event in history.

Apart from the early 1930s, much that has been written in the second part of the twentieth century has tended to be repetitious because it is part of women's social history, and an avalanche of books followed the American Bicentenary celebrations. In the 1980s most of the states in the United States of America ran huge projects, often state-funded, to document their old quilts, and from these projects also came books telling of the history of the quilts and quilters they had documented and photographed. Some of these documentation days unearthed often-forgotten techniques and local historical events, adding further to this fascinating part of feminine history and the mystique of the quilt.

I had already, from the mid-1970s, been endeavouring to document and photograph the old New Zealand quilts, which is why when I made my first trip to the United States and Canada in 1983 I received so much support from my friends there who were in the planning stages of their projects. It is now impossible to sort out the precise source for some of the facts presented in this book: whether it was the written word or conversations with other people interested in the subject. If anyone feels I have infringed on or plagiarised their writing, please be assured that this is completely unintentional.

Historical Books Used for Reference

Churchill, Winston. *The Island Race.* London: Cassell & Co. Ltd., 1964.

Hursthouse, Charles. *New Zealand, the Britain of the South.* London: Edward Stanford, 1861.

Joblin, Dorothea. *Behold The Plains — The Story of the Old Houses of Massey.* Auckland: Longman Paul Ltd., 1970.

McLintock, A.H. (ed). *An Encyclopaedia of New Zealand* (3 vols). Wellington: R.E. Owen, Government Printer, 1966.

Spencer, Margaret K. *Let Us Not Falter — The Spencer Pioneering Days.* Gisborne: Margaret K. Spencer, 1979.

British Quilts

Colby, Avril. *Patchwork.* London: B.T. Batsford Ltd., 1958.

Colby, Avril. *Quilting.* London: B.T. Batsford Ltd., 1972.

Osler, Dorothy. *Traditional British Quilts.* London: B.T. Batsford Ltd., 1987.

Irish Patchwork 1800–1900 (Exhibition catalogue). Allied Irish
Banks and Kilkenny Design Workshops, 1979.
[This is a splendid photographic catalogue with excellent commentaries, which accompanied a 1979 exhibition of quilts sponsored by Allied Irish Banks and Kilkenny Design Workshops. The exhibition also travelled to England and was shown at Somerset House, London in 1980.]

French Quilts

Berenson, Kathryn. *Quilts of Provence — The Art and Craft of French Quiltmaking.* London: Thames & Hudson Ltd., 1966.

Old American Quilts

Betterton, Sheila. *More Quilts & Coverlets, from the American Museum in Britain.* Bath: The American Museum in Britain, 1989.

Betterton, Sheila. *Quilts & Coverlets, from the American Museum in Britain.* Bath: The American Museum in Britain, 1978.

Bishop, Robert, and Safanda, Elizabeth. *A Gallery of Amish Quilts.* New York: E.P. Dutton & Co., Inc., 1983.

Eanes, Ellen Fickling et al., *North Carolina Quilts.* Chapel Hill, North Carolina: University of North Carolina Press, 1988.

Finley, Ruth E. *Old Patchwork Quilts and the Women who Made Them.* Massachusetts: Charles T. Branford Co., 1929; reprinted 1970.

Hall, Carrie A., and Kretsinger, Rose G. *The Romance of the Patchwork Quilt in America.* New York: Bonanza Books, a Division of Crown Publishers Inc., 1935.

Houck, Carter, and Miller, Myron. *American Quilts and How to Make Them.* New York: Charles Scribner's & Sons, 1975.

Oliver, Celia Y. *Enduring Grace — Quilts from the Shelbourne Museum Collection.* Lafayette, CA: C & T Publishing, 1997.

Orlofsky, Patsy & Myron. *Quilts in America.* McGraw-Hill Book Co., 1974; reprint edition New York: Abbeville Press, Inc.,1992.

Pottinger, David. *Quilts from the Indiana Amish.* New York: E.P. Dutton, Inc., in association with the Museum of American Folk Art, 1983.

Index

The American Quilt Study Group

The many volumes of research papers produced annually by The American Quilt Study Group under the title *Uncoverings* (edited by Sally Garoutte, a member of the group) are also a great source of information. This very learned group of women individually have also contributed articles to *Lady's Circle Patchwork Quilts* and *Quilters Newsletter*.

Horton, Laurel (ed.) *Quiltmaking in America — Beyond the Myths*. Selected writings from the American Quilt Study Group. Nashville, Tennessee: Rutledge Hill Press, 1994.

The articles published in *Lady's Circle Patchwork Quilts* magazine by Carter Houck when she was editor, and later as a columnist for the magazine *Quilters Newsletter* have been invaluable. Also valuable over the years have been articles in both these magazines written by Cuesta Ray Benberry, Barbara Brackman, Erma Kirkpatrick and Ruth Roberson, to name a few.

Some blocks made by New Zealand POWs and easily recognised by New Zealand quilters may be seen in photographs of the Changi quilts which accompanied Margaret Rolf's excellent article 'The Changi Quilts' in *Australian Patchwork & Quilting* Vol. 4 No. 2, 1997.